LETTERS

FROM

MY BROTHERS

TRANITA A. RANDOLPH STEPHENS

DEDICATION

This book is dedicated first and foremost to my Lord and Savior Jesus Christ. Every time I feel as if I am done with something......He speaks to me and as we all know when He speaks we must be obedient. This book is an assignment that He has given me. It is not written just for you, my readers, or the individuals who share their stories, nor the lives that I hope will be touched, but it is written for His glory.

To my wonderful daughters Tranisce and Trashawn, my hope is that I have beaten the less trodden path for you to travel down with minimal obstacles. To my sons Rodney and Rodell may you continue to rest peacefully in life everlasting and know that you both still inspire me to this day. To my granddaughters Tranae and Trinity always remember that you can stand on the shoulders of those before you to reach greater heights. To my grandsons Aidan and Jaxsen, remember to never ever allow anyone to tell you that you are not able. My parents, Leonard, and Corliss, I truly hope you are looking down from heaven and smiling with pride. To my aunt Gwen and uncle Permus, I thank you for always encouraging and believing in me.

Thank you to my surrogate aunts/godmothers, Becky Mays-Jenkins, Callie Terrell, and Cecelia Mayden for being there for me whenever your phone rang. Each family member through blood and marriage, your encouraging words mean the world to me. Hugs and kisses to all of you. To my loving, kindhearted husband Ralph aka Weasel, what can I say? You have supported, encouraged, and loved on me in every aspect that anyone could. Thank you and I will love you always.

To all of my past, present and future readers, thank you. I hope this piece of work gives you an understanding of any situation that was beyond your control. I pray that if there are any similarities in any of these stories with what you have endured in life, that you allow God to guide you to find forgiveness and peace.

INTRODUCTION

As women we make mistakes. We do and say things that can be not only hurtful to us but to our family and friends. Yet, as time moves on and we make changes to our lives and amends to those that we have harmed, we anticipate forgiveness. We look forward to emotional and mental support to help us get to our next level. Most times we receive it and others we do not.

Thinking about society but mainly women, we gather around one another and provide that support and encouragement that we seek from one another. Whether it is to genuinely help us be better mothers, sisters, aunts, or grandmothers. We as women falter, fall, and either get up on our own or have our village pick us up. We give a tremendous number of accolades when we see each other striving and achieving milestones in our individual lives.

I know there have been countless times that I have said or heard another woman say, "congratulations" on your child winning the trophy, making the honor roll, graduations, the birth of a child, a new job and so on. Granted there are a number of times where that woman has done a lot of it by herself, without the help of the biological father of her child. It is a very well-known and unfortunate scenario that we have seen played out repeatedly throughout time.

The lyrics of a certain well known artist chants out in a chorus "who runs the world (girls), who runs the world (girls)." With the hands of time turned back, it has always been the female population that took care of the children while most husbands went out to earn a living. This left the mother in charge of the home, having to make most of the decisions regarding rearing the children. As years go by, it became commonplace to see a wife/mother transitioning from just being a stay-at-home mom to a working mom who also ran the house, took care of the children, and made all the decisions. Typically, it was because the husband, dad, father, or breadwinner was no longer in the picture holding up his end of the responsibilities. He, for whatever reason, could be found anywhere else but in the home. Now don't get things twisted and get angry. I am not saying it was each family that felt this shift in their household composition. However, the numbers started growing more and more through the years.

Have you ever stopped and asked yourself why was this breakdown happening in many families? There was never just one reason. It could have been lack of work, the inability to communicate, mental health issues, physical or substance abuse, or even the mere fact that there was no one that showed these individuals how to be men.

Before proceeding with reading, ask yourself these questions. What about the men that stayed there? What about the one's that faltered, fell, and didn't get up? Or those that eventually got up on their own after dragging themselves through the mud or battling their own demons?

What is it about what we see as a society that when a man falls, or does not do what he should do as a parent versus when that same scenario happens with women? Why are we so much more forgiving of women when they get themselves together and manage their business and not our men? Does it not sometimes take as much for a man to pull himself up by his bootstraps to get back on track as it takes for a woman? What about the mother that decides to leave and make the decision that being a hands-on mother is not what she thought it was cut out to be? Thus, leaving the child or children in the total care of a father or another relative? Does that mother get a pass for her behavior? Does she get treated by society as we tend to treat absent fathers?

I know someone is saying there is a difference between a father and a daddy. Absolutely! So, what would be the difference between a mother and a mommy? Should we say the same thing? If so, then shouldn't the fathers and dads get those same type of congratulatory wishes for the progresses that he was able to achieve on his own without the help of a biological mother present? However, there appears to be a slight tip of the scale when it comes to our male counterparts.

Often it is the father that gets the "dead beat" stigmatism placed on his life for his lack of participation and hands on rearing of his children. Some may not deserve it but then there are a number of men who do.

On the other hand, there are some men who did not jump ship. They stayed in the trenches to raise their children along with the mother. Whether it was a wife, long-term girlfriend, or baby mama, they remained constant. They showed up like they were supposed to. That brings me back to the question I asked earlier. Do these men receive the same parental accolades that we bestow upon women? Or do we just whisper "he's doing what he is supposed to do." Well, isn't a mother doing what she is supposed to do when we lift her up in all the glories of positive parenting?

I have spoken to a number of men from various social, economic, and educational backgrounds from at least five states who have shared their stories with me about their ups, downs, disappearing acts, lack of presence and anything else you could use to summarize their "less than stellar participation in their role of fathering their children." While shedding the light on some individuals' negative and challenging plights, I was also able to speak with some men who have been on the opposite side and have maintained a front and center position in the lives of their offspring. Stay with me here and allow the men in this book to tell their story. Why they stayed, why they left, and how they perceive themselves and others as being an intricate part of their lives.

RELEASE OF INFORMATION

Each chapter in this book stems from a true story. The characters are fictitious names chosen strictly by the individual sharing his experience(s) as a parent.

Video recordings, interviews and all levels of communication were made individually to keep everyone separate (no one knows whatever male parent is in any chapter). The recordings were transcribed by me and then shared with everyone separately before going to print to ensure all facts (as they shared) were correct to the best of their recollection.

TABLE OF CONTENTS

I was born and raised in the North. I had a happy and stable childhood. I was raised in the household by my mom along with one sister. My sister and I had the same mother but different fathers. I dropped out of high school and felt that I needed to get away from the area. So, when I was sixteen, I attended job corp. I was there for two years and received my driver's license, my GED and a plumbing and electrician trade certificate. While there I thought about attending college but opted out of that opportunity. It was good for me to be on my own even in that structured environment for a little while. My family was also very supportive during this phase of my life.

MEMORIES

My mother didn't have a lot of male friends, but the ones that she did have, I could understand that my mom was lonely. That made her make some hasty decisions, but I don't fault her for it. Like my sister's father, he was supposedly Muslim. My sister has a Muslim name. Somehow before he became Muslim, he was abusive towards my mother.

His parents lived across the street from my grandmother. They separated and once he found out my mother had another boyfriend, then he became really aggressive. He broke into our house. He pulled the pipes out of the wall, and he confronted my mother and her boyfriend at one point, and they got into an altercation. I don't know the details of that because I was young, but I do remember that happening. So, the boyfriend that she had, he kind of pulled away because he didn't want to get involved with this. So, this left my mother alone again and she just continued the cycle of picking the wrong men. She eventually picked one man and we moved. We were living in one area, and she moved us further out to another.

My mom wanted to give us a better life by moving out of the apartment and into a house in a more rural area with better schools instead of a city setting. We moved in with a man, but it didn't work out. He wound up leaving us in his house, which my mother couldn't afford to maintain. So, we ended up moving back into the apartment. Once we moved back, he started coming around again. By then, my mom was working six days a week to provide for us. My mom said he (the guy we had moved into the house with), was coming around and that on one occasion she had talked to him outside of the apartment, he had a gun. We didn't think anything of it. On one Saturday she was going to work, and he shot my mom three times. Actually, I heard the last shot. I looked out the window and he was standing over my mother. He looks up at me and he shot himself in the head right in front of me. What I later found out was he had been diagnosed with Leukemia and was dying and he wanted my mom to die along with him. By the grace of God my mom survived the shooting and is still living. I don't think my mom has had a solid relationship with anyone after that.

EMOTIONAL RESIDUE

As I grew up after witnessing my mom go through a devastating chain of events in life, I changed the way I interacted with both her and my sister. I became more protective of both of them. After that, I didn't approve of anyone she brought around us.

Eventually we moved from up north to a little south in a different state, where my mom was born and raised. My mom comes from a large family that bore children from the same parentage. Therefore, it affords me an extensive family from her side.

I have never met my biological father and never knew his name. My mom never spoke of him. I was never told anything about him. Not one thing was shared with me. I don't know what the situation was with him or about them. I could only speculate. Maybe he was married or something like that. I don't know.

Later in life, when I was about in my 20's, my uncle realized that I had never met the man who was supposed to be my biological father. He actually knew him, and he told me his name. Once I found out his name, I never pursued it or him. My mom with all that she had going on, I just wanted to support her. I just wanted to be by her side. Whatever decisions she made, I stuck by her.

BECOMING A FATHER

Not knowing who my father was while I was growing up left a mark of sheer determination on my life. By not knowing him or having any idea who he was, I was determined to be the best father I could possibly be.

I don't care what happened between my kids and their mothers, I was always going to be in my kids' life. This is the effect of not having a father in my life growing up. I don't care if my kids were out of the country, I was going to have a relationship with them.

I have five uncles and having them along with different situations in life has given me a combination of how I learned to be a father. Three uncles up North, I had contact with growing up but the two that lived in the South were not in contact with me during this time for me to learn or pick up certain things from them as a young man. Overall, none of them were involved in teaching me how to be a parent, I mostly picked it up from my mom.

I was over twenty-one years old, single, and never married, when I found out I was going to be a father. Being responsible for another person besides myself was a little scary. With my oldest son, I met his mother when she was already pregnant (which I did not know immediately). Once she revealed to me that she was in fact carrying a child, I had doubts due to the timing if the unborn child was mine or not. She was dealing with her own drug habit, so I just decided to take him from her. I didn't care if he was mine or not. I knew that he needed somebody. I knew what it was like to grow up without a father and I just didn't want to see him grow up like that. My mom and I decided to raise him as our own. Later in life, I found out that he was not my son, but by then it didn't matter. The relationship between his mother and I dwindled out over time. She found herself involved in the court system and had to serve a sentence. My mom helped me out a lot and I raised him.

In my late twenties, I had two children with another woman. We were living together at one point. After a while, we ended up separating and then she calls me one day and tells me to "come get the kids." At the time I was living in a one-bedroom apartment with my oldest son, yet I went and picked up my other two children. I had been paying child support to her for my two children. So, naturally I went to the courts, had the custody order reversed and received full custody of my children. As a mother, she didn't put up any type of fight to keep her children in her custody. So, I raised the two of them on my own as well.

I received custody of my kids when they were very young. My daughter was about three years old, and my son was less than a year old. My first son, from my previous relationship, was about five years old at that time. So, I am looking at a five-year-old, a three-year-old, and a baby under one year of age and I am raising them in a one-bedroom apartment. I ended up having to stay at this apartment because I was unable to break my lease. Once the appropriate time came where my lease was up, I was able to obtain Section 8 housing and moved in another place with my three children. There was no co-parenting with the mother of my children. At some point she decided that she didn't want to take on the responsibilities of being a mother. Once again, it was me and my mom.

Time moved on and I ended up being in a relationship with another woman. This was not the end of my pro-creating. It was not a planned pregnancy. I was in my late thirties and another child was not something that I wanted. I didn't want to be a parent at that time because I felt that I was too old, and I didn't want to cheat the child out of their childhood by being an older person trying to raise it. I eventually had another son. His mom and I were living in Section 8 housing together. We lived together for about six years, and we eventually separated. There was a period when she lived with me, and she was trying to get herself together. She relocated to another state and tried to establish herself there. I kept my youngest son who was about five years old at the time with me for about ten months when she decided to return and get him.

With my ex coming to take my son to another state to live with her I had to channel my feelings and keep in mind that it wasn't about me it was about my son. I knew that he missed his mom. Yes, I would have preferred to keep him, but I sent him with his mother. Eventually they moved back home to the South. She felt that she did not have family support in the other state. I always maintained a relationship with my son, even when he was in another state. I would talk to him over the phone and even went to visit him twice. They were in that state for about three years I believe. I made sure during that time I was available to my son. Whether it was to talk on the phone, go down to see him, financially, and emotionally. I have always felt like his mother should never have to tell anyone to tell me how to take care of my kid. When she asked for anything concerning my son, I had sprung into action like a superhero.

The hardest thing I have had to learn to deal with as a parent has been watching them make mistakes. My two oldest boys were always active and hanging out in the neighborhood. Eventually they wound up getting into trouble which in turn landed them in jail. I tried to set them a good example. I went to work, and I have had the same job for eighteen years. However, you know the old saying "you can lead a horse to water, but you can't make them drink." I wanted them to be their own people. I can't hold their hand through life for them.

My biggest challenge was just trying to work and spending time with my kids. As a single parent it is difficult. You worry about the streets, or TV or anything else having a big influence on your children. You should be the biggest influence in your kid's life. If you are not putting in the time, it's hard.

At one point I got caught up in making sure they had everything but realizing at one point all they wanted was me to spend time with them. So, I had to kind of balance that out. I made the sacrifice of not hanging out with my friends as much or going out. I invited my friends over to my house instead of going over to their house.

My biggest thing is don't try to be a best friend with your kids. They already have friends. They need a parent. They need somebody to call them out when they're wrong. Explain to them instead of just yelling at them or hitting them. Yes. Explain to them what they are doing is wrong. Just try to talk to them and just have patience. God, I had to learn that. I had to learn patience in being a parent. That was my biggest thing.

So, my words of wisdom are the same things I tell my kids and that is, "you can't go wrong by doing the right thing." As long as you are doing the right thing you cannot go wrong.

There are a lot of young men out here that are taking care of their kids. They need to realize that they have just as many rights to their child as the mother does and a lot of men don't exercise their rights. Even if you don't have money, it doesn't cost anything to give yourself.

"T.J."

I did not have both of my parents in my household as I was growing up. My mom was there raising me, and my father was absent. I did not have any siblings and my grandmother and grandfather were in the house with us as well.

My childhood was partially happy when I was younger. With that being said, it's somewhat confusing for me to say whether my childhood was happy or sad. I would ask questions about things and would not get the answers I expected or any answer at all. One, if not the most frequent question I would ask was "where's my father."

Being the only child, I would come downstairs on Christmas morning, and look under the tree, and you know that 85%-95% of the presents was yours but once you get older you want to know. You see everybody with a mother and father, and you ask about yours, the subject is intentionally changed. When I mentioned my father, it was taboo, and the subject was immediately changed. They would switch it to something else or bribe me to stop talking about it. For the most part, I can say I had more of a strict childhood than anything. As I look back, I realize that I was more sheltered than everybody else as I was growing up.

I did not know my father from birth. I think I was around five or six years old when I met him. He came to the house, and I did not know who he was. My grandmother looked at me and said, "this is your father." My response was, "oh okay." It wasn't like me running to him and jumping into his arms and stuff like that because I didn't know who this dude was, you say he is my father, but I didn't know where the hell he had been.

21

As I was growing up, he would come around, but he was more like one of the homies. He wasn't really, I guess like a traditional father was. He would come by some time. I remember once, I was out playing, and he came there and as I got home there were all of these police officers and he is outside with my mom arguing. He grabbed onto me, grabbed my mom's arm and he wouldn't let go. I really didn't understand a whole lot of what was going on. I was just a kid and had no clue what was what. I did ask my mom what it was all about, and she just told me not to worry about it, just go get yourself together, go take a bath and get ready to go to bed. I remember it being the summertime. During the summer I would spend time with my mom when I was not in school because during the school year I was with my grandmother. I would only see my mom on the weekend during that time because she worked.

In a way, I felt kind of abandoned when I was a kid because I only saw my mom on those weekends. I didn't understand that my father had left, took everything, and left her with nothing. Of course, that left her to struggle to pay $150 a month for a two-bedroom apartment back in the '70s. My grandmother used to get up in the mornings, walk several miles to catch the bus and she would get off and stand and wait. The bus would come by, and my mom would hand me off to my grandmother as she stood on the bottom step of the bus and then she would go on to work. This went on for years until I was old enough to go to school and that was when my grandmother told my mom to "just leave the boy here" and that is when I started going to school. That is how it came to be that I only saw my mother on the weekends and not seeing my father.

By the time I was ten or eleven years old, my father started to show his face again. He would never come to my mom's house. He would come to my grandmother's house. I am not sure if it were preplanned or arranged but he would never come to my grandmother's house when my mom or any of my uncles were around. It was a known fact to everyone but me that my uncles (my mother's brothers) couldn't stand my father. They never told me, but I found out later why and what was going on. My father had problems.

My parents got married in either 1962 or 1963 and a couple of years later I was born in 1965. I actually have pictures of their wedding. However, there are no memories really of the early part of them because he was gone by the time, I was five years old. He and I never did anything together. He showed up one day with a bike he had purchased. Some of the toys that I used to have, I always thought they had come from my grandparents and my mom. There were a couple of racetracks that I think he bought that my mother never let me play with. Never. They stayed on the shelf until I was old enough and then she said I was too big for them and gave them away. They were brand new, and she had never let me take them out of the box. She would tell me how I "bet 'not touch it; if I catch you touching it, I will beat your x$$." Now thinking about it, it probably came from him, and she didn't want me to have it.

MEMORIES

There are a lot of stories that I found out about later. For one, my father used to hang at this spot on a corner where you could party on a popular street in my hometown where they had barber shops and whatever else you needed there or at the pool hall. My parents were living here in my grandmother's house. From what I understand, I guess my mom was reluctant to tell me this. When I was younger, he came home from his extracurricular activities and being a man, he wanted relations and my mom said no and he said yeah and nine months later I was born. When she told me that, I thought to myself, was I an accident or something? Sometimes I think my mom felt some type of way because maybe at that time things were getting worse. I don't know how bad they were, but my grandfather broke my father's arm. I don't know if he said something to my grandmother or if he was trying to do something to my mother, but he (my grandfather) snapped my father's arm like a twig. I know at least two of my uncles made it known that they wanted to do something to my dad (I don't know, they may have). During it all though, nobody said anything to me about my father. It was a downright forbidden subject.

When I became a teenager, I think I was seventeen, my father and I were walking up 14th Street. There was a house that we went to, and a lady came outside and told me that my last name was not what I knew it to be and that it was another name. I remember this day so vividly, including what she looked like and what she was wearing. About two years after my mom had passed away, I was going through her possessions, and I found the paperwork where my father petitioned the Court to change his last name. I was already here. I was three years old when he did it. Nobody ever told me the reason behind it. All of that bothers me to this day. It makes me always question who I am. I know nothing of my father's side of the family. I don't know any medical conditions that he may have had. I just don't know anything because he killed himself. It was 1986 and he was in a house, when he locked himself in a bedroom and set it on fire and died of smoke inhalation.

My most memorable negative memory from my childhood was the way the other kids treated me. They thought that because I was the only child that I was spoiled. Even though a lot of times that is the case, it was not that way in my family.

My most memorable positive memory of my childhood was the first time I dunked a basketball when I was in the sixth grade. I was outside and we were using a kickball. I had the ball, bounced it, and went for it.

There were a few solid men in my life that I had good connections with. One in particular was the Chief in a police department who my mom dated. He understood what was going on at the time. I can only assume that my mom told him about what was going on with my father. He would come by with his complete uniform on with his stars and weapon. Sometimes he would take me to McDonald's. He would always tell me to "mind my mama" and talk about education. Eventually he moved on. Then there was another man, and he would teach me things about cars and tools. He would tell me to hand him the small, medium, or large tool and I had to learn what measurement it was. I would go with him to the racetrack because he was part of a pit crew. It made me feel involved because I used to think he was the kind of dad that I would want. One thing I will never forget was when night came, they would take me down on the track. They had to put earphones on me because I was just that close to one of the dragsters. Back then, the engines would sit up in front of the driver. So, I am sitting there feeling the thunder in my chest and even with headphones on I can still hear the loud noises. I could clearly see the flames jumping out of the pipes, along with the Christmas tree (where they start the race). It was red, yellow, yellow, green and I blinked. The car was sitting there, then I looked down at the track and it was a dot. It was there one second and a dot the next. I was seven years old, and it was game over after that. That's how I realized I had a passion for speed which eventually led me to working on cars.

Those were the main two guys that I remember in my life that I remember from when I was young that left a solid impact on my life. In addition to them I also received life lessons from certain family members if not by a direct but an indirect action. My maternal uncles, maternal aunt, and her husband, as well as a maternal first cousin. These individuals showed me by their walk in their lives what to do, not do and how I could handle certain situations within marriage whenever I got to that point. It's like you learn something in school and you feel that you will never need to use it in life. Not knowing how you will use it then does not negate the fact that you learned it. The time when you get to that point in your life will definitely take your memory back to the lesson in remembering how you saw others close to you deal with the situation. So those individuals deposited more into me than any of them could ever imagine.

BECOMING A FATHER

I believe I was a sophomore in high school, about sixteen or seventeen years old when I found out that I was going to be a father. My initial thoughts were that my mother was going to kill me, so I never told her. It was more of a fly by night type of thing between the girl and me. Actually, she came on to me and it just happened. After our encounter I didn't see her for a long time. Well, actually I would see her, but she was always wearing this coat and I didn't care if it were two hundred degrees outside, she had on the coat. I later realized that it was because she was hiding the fact that she was pregnant. I didn't know anything about it. I just knew that she was avoiding me. I don't think that she wanted the baby or even wanted the whole pregnancy to happen. It wasn't until one day that I was walking into the first building at our school, and she was coming out of the building with some of her girlfriends and she had this baby in the stroller. The baby looked like me, but there was also another dude in school that everybody thought that we were brothers.

In reality, to this day, I don't know if that child is mine or not. Her mother did not like me, but I would go over there. I guess because I had dishonored her family and her child, and she just didn't like me. At that point I was just a boy so what did she think I knew about being a father? I was still living at home with my mother, and I didn't know anything about a kid, buying pampers, formula or none of that. So, I brought soda and potato chips when I came. That's all I knew. I didn't know anything. I do remember the day that I went over there, and she met me at the door, and she looked me in my face and said, "I don't approve of you; I don't like you; you ain't never gonna amount to nothing; and we don't need you." She then slammed the door in my face. That was the last time I saw my child until she was twenty-one years old. They just disappeared. She had a best friend who I would ask about her whereabouts, but she could never truly tell me anything. I had no way of making any calls. She should have been in school, but her mother shipped her somewhere else.

I did not know that my daughter's mother had gone to prison for about ten years. I don't really talk to her, and I really do not have a relationship with my daughter. If she is mine. I will say that I have tried to reach out to her at times. The only time she would call is when she needs money. When my mother died, she made no effort to come up here from where I knew her to be living. If she had wanted to come up, I would have made a way for her and the kids to do so. She didn't want to do that, but she did ask about the house and wanted to know what I was going to do with it.

I haven't really said anything to her but from what I understand, I now have a great-grandson. My daughter has six children, and my granddaughter has a son. I try to message them, but I get no responses at all. So, at this point my thoughts are if it's like that, then it's like that. I try not to constantly worry about it. I think that if I had told my mother initially when this happened, I think my daughter's life would have been a little different. My mom would have really been involved in it and maybe she wouldn't have had all of these kids. Each one of her kids has a different father. Maybe it would have changed the course of my life as well. I don't know. I think about them all the time.

My other daughter brings me back to the question of whether she is my child as well. She was born from my first marriage. I was at work one day and social services called me up. Basically, they just said to me, "hey, guess what; you have a daughter." Now, I'm at work thinking, "what??" Naturally, I kind of laughed it off and told them to stop playing. During that conversation I found out that the child's mother said that I was the father of the newborn. The information that was provided to me was that she was at a bus stop and went into labor right there. After she had the baby, they asked her who the father was, and I was named. The funny part (or not) is that we weren't living together as husband and wife at that time.

Knowing that it only takes one time, but I never knew. I was in no condition at that time to take care of anybody. I was barely taking care of myself. So, I had to do what was best. I gave her up for adoption. At this time, I was maybe twenty-two or twenty-three years old when that happened. When I say I was in no condition to be a parent, I was in the streets doing all types of crazy mess.

I was married to her for about two years. The doubt of me being my child's father or not came into play because I was not around. My wife at the time and I were not kicking it. Neither of us were in our right mind. All I can say is when

Rick James said that cocaine was a helluva drug, he wasn't lying. So, with that being the basis of our entire being at that time, there was more than enough grounds for me to be uncertain as to whether or not I was the father.

The last thing that I can recall, my daughter was staying with her adoptive parents. I mean, if I were to walk pass her, I wouldn't know who she was. Unlike my oldest daughter, when I saw her, I knew exactly whose she was. I kind of messed her up with that one day. I hadn't seen her since she was six years old and when she was twenty-one, I walked into a store and I saw her and I was like, "I'll be damned!" I walked up to her and said "hello" and she looked at me. She didn't know who I was until I told her. I just blurted out, "I'm your father." Then her mother found out that we met. Later her grandmother (the one who slammed the door in my face), found out and then it was just like history repeated itself all over again.

My third child is my son who was born from a "friends with benefits" situation. Once again, I did not know until I was told, "oh by the way let me tell you this since we are having a conversation." He was already here by the time I found out and about three years old. His mom nor I knew how to get in contact with one another and just ran into each other one day. I was able to see him once and have not seen him again since. He basically does not know that I exist. So, I do not have any type of relationship with him at all.

I have not seen nor spoken to his mom. I do know that she was involved with someone either during the time we were dealing with one another or shortly after. That person is who has taken on the role of daddy because she was in love with him. So, my son has grown up believing that another man is his father. I allowed myself to be okay with the situation because they had already become a family and did not deserve to have their lives disrupted. It would have just caused chaos in a family, and they did not need it.

I have been married to my current wife for twenty-two years. She does have a son. He has seen me at my worst in growing up around me. He is a great young man and has just recently gotten married. I remember as he was growing up the two of us used to play basketball together. He would always get upset at me because I would never let him win. It was an ego thing, but it also helped to build sportsmanship in him. He and I do talk. When he has a problem or need to talk, he will call me up. His conversation may start with "Pop maaaaan…." And it is at that time I know something is going on and he needs to vent. I allow him to get it all of his chest to get some relief and give me some understanding of what's going on and then I gladly step up to provide him with my take on it without trying to push him in one direction or another but allowing him to make a sound, respectful and mature decision on the matter at hand.

REGRETS

The regret that I have in my parenting is the fact that I didn't know how to do it. I really didn't have anyone to talk to about it. If there had been someone that I could have seriously sat down with and told them that I had a kid, or I don't know what to do because I'm just a boy myself. That would have been a big help to me. Seeing the struggle of what it was like for parents in my family. It may have looked easy for me as a child because for the most part I didn't want for anything. I may not have gotten what I wanted right then and there, but somehow, someway; a way was made. We got it. We had food, clothes, and shelter but when you are a kid you really aren't thinking about it. You're being selfish saying, "I want this," "I want that." Just because some other child has it so now that means you want it. What you don't realize is that if my mom or dad buys this then the light bill may not get paid, or you may not get the frosted flakes that you like. As a child you don't think about do you want a toy or do you want to eat. Now as I am older, I realize that the struggle is real. So that is one thing that if I could turn back the hands of time, maybe if I had found someone to confide in but there was basically nobody there.

WORDS OF WISDOM

There is a problem that has been affecting a good portion of our families. I, myself was a part of the same problem. That is a number of us lack certain guidance, morals, and standards. I truly believe that a woman is the best person to teach their daughter. A man is the perfect one that teaches the son. I also believe that the man should be there for his daughters as well to let these young ladies know that there are predators out there and they are going to tell you everything just to get with you. Some of the ladies that I have dealt with had daughters and I have chased boys off. I had to tell them "yeah, I know why you are here. You ain't slick; I was your age. Do you think you are doing something new? No. We did it before you and our parents did too."

Even though I didn't grow up with a father in the house, back then there were many households that had fathers that went to work and came home. It wasn't until the lates '70s and '80s that everything just went haywire and has gotten worse with each generation. I haven't heard one person say 'yes ma'am' or 'no ma'am' in years. That in itself was the first thing that used to come out of our mouth when a person that was older than us was addressing us. It was instilled in us to always say 'yes ma'am' and 'no sir.' If not, then there was a hand, a belt, a switch, a tree limb, or something that would come out of nowhere and make contact with you and/or your mouth. Even the absence of respect in speaking to someone

31

and not addressing them as Mr., Mrs., Miss has gone astray. The level of respect in speaking to someone elder than you has diminished drastically. We were taught to never ever call our parents, aunts, grandparents, and any of their friends by their first names. You just didn't do that.

In closing I want to say to the young men coming behind me is to not get caught up in certain lifestyles that you know are bad just to be a part of. If you feel some type of way like I did, I was shy and had a thing for the stars (I was really different), and I really didn't fit in. I wasn't accepted by everybody else. In order to be accepted or fit in I had to do what they did, which I did not like, and I definitely paid the ultimate price for it throughout the years. Don't let anything deter you from what you want to be. You are who you are. Stay away from bad people or the ones that claim to be your friends but really are not. You know who they are and are not.

As far as parenting is concerned, there are no instructions for it. You will have to make it work as you go through it. Think about your future first and definitely think about planned parenthood. For one, babies are not cheap, and you have to remember at all times that you have a child that you have to be responsible for. Regardless of what you are going through do not let the child suffer because you and the child's mom are not getting along. This is a serious scenario that we see all the time. Whatever is going on between the two of you has no bearing whatsoever on the need for love and care for the child.

Always have some respect and dignity for yourself. Don't get caught up in the mix of what's going on. Stay in school and get your education because it will definitely pay off one day. Staying away from the gangs and the negative stuff that you already know means you no good from the start. If there is something that you don't have, don't blame others, just make a plan, and go out and be whatever you feel you need to be in order to achieve those goals. You will have to earn it because no one is giving you anything. The only thing that you will get for free is a hard time and a fast way to get it. Once you go out and earn something that you want, you will find yourself more appreciative of it than if someone had just given it to you. The thing of when someone just gives you something, they will remind you as often as you allow them.

So just remember to take your time in making your decisions that can permanently affect your life. You have one life, and you don't want to spend half of it wasting your time and thoughts on regrets.

"JOE"

GROWING UP

Both of my parents were present in the household when I was growing up. They were married for thirty-five years. I would like to think I had a spectacular childhood with parents that created a very good home setting. The only thing that was required of me was to do what I was told to do. I had to go to school and do whatever I was told to do in school, and I was rewarded with the things that I asked for. I appreciated my mother and father for who they were, and I never had any problems with them because I respected them, therefore they respected me. I give credit to this because of the era I came up in.

There were certain things that were not allowed, and one of the main ones was no back talking. I did get a couple of beatings, but they were deserved. There were only a handful of them in my entire childhood. Back in the day, my parents were able to talk to me or should I say, give me a stern talking to and that look. That infamous look could mean anything from, "shut up," "keep your mouth shut" or any other directive to straighten you up. When we went out to dinner, I would get that talk before going into the restaurant. They would simply say, "you know what to do," "go in here and act like you know," and there wouldn't be a problem when we leave there. Overall, I can't complain about my childhood.

I have two older sisters who are twelve and ten years older than me. They had a different father than I did. I never knew their father, so there was never any interaction between he and I. Being the baby of the three of us, I was spoiled. However, I didn't push my luck on assuming that I would get everything that I wanted. I did earn what I wanted as well.

The most negative memory I have that has impacted my life was my parents' divorce. Even though I was an adult, it still sticks with me today. Even with both of them being deceased, it still bothers me. It does so because I have never been able to get any real clarification as to how and why it happened. The subject never came up between my father and me. Even after the divorce, I was still treated the same way. I did forgive my father, especially knowing that there is no clear path to heaven if you have not forgiven people for what you feel are their wrongdoings. My father eventually relocated while my mother continued to stay here close by until she passed away.

In speaking on my most positive memory, it would have to be during my high school era. I was allowed to drive to school every day after taking my father to work. I would call that being a responsible person at my age then. My parents trusted me a lot so that was always a positive for me.

I have a great bond with my siblings. One resides in this area where I reside while the other is in another state down south. My relationship with them allows me to be able to have a daily conversation with them and this helps us to constantly grow and love on one another. My siblings gave me a lot of respect and trust as I was growing up too. They kept me sharp and took good care of me as well by purchasing things for me. When I was younger, I had an account set up when I was in high school that I used to go and buy clothes for school, and they knew I was responsible enough to go in and order clothes on my own. We got along well and never had any problems.

I did well in school and graduated. There were few options given to me by parents pertaining to school. It was always said to me, 'you will graduate.' I wanted to go to a trade school to be a mechanic but my mother for some reason didn't want me to go. When I left high school, I worked jobs that allowed me to work outside, which I prefer to do. However, I did work a government job indoors for about two years but that ended up not being for me. I ended up settling into a driving position within the transit system where I gave them twenty-eight years of dedicated service. I have been retired now for about eight years.

BECOMING A FATHER

I was twenty-two years old when I found out I was going to be a father. My initial emotion was of shock in the beginning. However, back in those days, I did not have a choice of being a "baby-daddy" as it is called today. I had to step up and marry this person at a young age. She and I had been in a relationship already for about six years prior to the pregnancy. I was not ready for marriage, but I did what needed to be done and maintained it. Altogether we had three children, a daughter and two sons (who are deceased). Our marriage lasted about eight years until we ended up getting divorced.

After my first wife and I had been separated for about two years, I had another child, a son, outside of the marriage. The relationship between myself and his mother of what would be my fourth child was not a healthy one. There were a number of brick walls and issues that I had to face. We were not living together, so that created an entirely different scenario for parenting. I was finding out as time went on that one of the biggest issues was not seeing eye to eye with someone who wanted to raise our child solo. There was a lot of push-back because our son's mother wanted to raise him the way she wanted to and was not flexible in hearing my opinion about things. This went on for the first sixteen years of his life until she found that he needed something that she could not give him. At that time, he was 'dropped' on my doorstep for a lack of a better word. At that age, there was not a great deal that I could do with him.

Naturally, the relationship between myself and my son was rocky because he felt as though I had never been in his life. I tried to explain to him that his mother did not want me in his life at that particular time and now you are sixteen and I'm supposed to 'raise you.' I had no contact with him at all, by his mother's choice, for those years. It was a difficult time, and it was strained. It was at that point that I had to introduce him to his three older siblings. They did not take it too well because, here I am bringing him around saying "this is your brother." Of course, initially, their first reactions were, "where did he come from?" There was a big adjustment period. What I did was get them all together on the weekends. I would take them out together to dinner so they could get to know one another and eventually it all worked itself out.

My daughter, who is my oldest child, still didn't take it as easy as her younger brothers did. Her thoughts were that by her being the oldest there was not going to be anyone else coming into the picture that consisted of her and her two brothers that had always been there. I understood. It was a hard pill to swallow to bring a stranger into the family and explain to them that this is your brother. They all were able to create bonds in their own ways. I did have a support system that included my mom and my two sisters. My mom would spend time with my daughter on the weekends and their bond became very strong. My mom definitely loved all of the kids, but she loved that first grandchild. My dad, as well, was a good support to me. He explained to me a lot about dealing with the situation. He made sure he reminded me to be smart with my thinking and never to react with my emotions.

After my son came to stay with me the communication with his mom and I did improve a little. The biggest drawback was that she would still try and tell me how to raise him. I didn't like that at all. How do you bring someone to your house after sixteen years and then expect to have your say in how he is raised? I constantly had to tell her that "what goes on in my house is in my house." In the same token, "what goes on in your house is your house." There are things that I am not going to tolerate and that's just the way it is.

As a father in the house, I feel as if I did good raising the kids. I was blessed to be able to work a full and part time job in the beginning. I also was able to purchase my first home at the age of twenty-four. To me that was a big accomplishment at my age. My first marriage went well until we had outside influences in the mix of our relationship. At one point, I thought I would see certain behaviors, but told myself that I wasn't. Only to find out later that these things were actually happening. In other words, my first wife was not as on top of the finances in our home because she was focused more on helping other households with their bills. Of course, that bothered me. I would ask her about it and did not receive a truthful answer. Being the provider that I knew how to be and learning this piece of information was not conducive to the way I was trying to build a life for us as a family. I did not step out on my marriage. I raised the children, and we were a close-knit family. We went to church together and always had dinner as a family afterward. Things were good.

My biggest challenge as a father was when we separated. I had to explain to the kids what was going on and I was told by them that I didn't love them anymore. They questioned me about the reasoning of my departure and leaving their mother. I could only explain to the best of my ability why I was in one place and yet their mother was over there. That was hard for them to grasp and understand because they had seen us together as a family for seven years in the same household.

During this time, I had just started a new job. I worked late nights and was not off on the weekends, it was tough. I would talk to the kids but not as much as I would have liked to. A few years down the road, I would somewhat be forced to be around and talk to the kids. Their mother would want to go somewhere, and she would drop them off with the explanation of having to go somewhere and she would be back and then leave them with me. It wasn't as if I had a problem with watching the kids, it was just that my work schedule was not what I felt it needed to be at the time. It actually took years before I was at the point where I could be off on the weekends to be able to spend more time with them. I used to work at night and shortly after I get home, about twelve or one o'clock in the morning, I couldn't spend time talking with them. We would get a chance to chat for a few minutes maybe three or four times per week. I can tell you that it was not like it was supposed to be.

GENERATIONAL TRAITS

Just as I was taught growing up, I have always asked my kids to respect me and my household. Although they are all grown now, that is something that is never going to change. If you don't respect my house, then you don't come here. It's that simple. They respect me, my house, and my wife of today. They have never treated her 'different.' They have never called her stepmom. It has always been mom. She has done the same with them. It has never been a step nothing or a bonus anything. They truly love one another, and I like that. Those are the most important things that I can say that I have taken with me from my upbringing to where I am now. Respect and love for everyone. Anything other than that I will not tolerate. Yes, we bump heads. That's natural, but that's normal with most families.

REGRETS

I always say to myself, that I wish I could have done some things differently. However, I was really upset with the kids' mother and the way she was doing things and would get under my skin and tear me down. I know that I took some things out on my kids that I should not have. Those things I wish I could take back, but those days are gone.

SOCIETY AND MY CHILDREN

I feel as if society may have played about fifty percent in the upbringing of my kids and their influences. My two boys really needed me in the house with them because they were out there. When I tried to talk to them, their mother interrupted and that played a part in things that I didn't like. My ability and right to be a father would always be shortchanged. I felt that I should still be able to be their father, even if I am not in the same household with them. If I see something that I feel is not right, then I am going to say something. However, with her, I had no right to say anything at all. I was just expected to pay the child support.

My daughter used to call and talk to me a lot. She would confide in me about a lot of things. One day I had a conversation with her mother explaining to her that since we were not together, I needed her to watch out for our daughter.

41

There were a couple of male members of her family that did not sit well with me, and I had a dislike for some of their ways. Eventually, everything that I had said to her about those individuals, did happen to my daughter.

There were a lot of outside people who always had something to say about what was going on in the household. They had no pertinent business and needed to just keep their opinions to themselves. I would attempt to talk to my ex-wife about the conversations that were being held with her and these outsiders and the reasoning behind them. When you have what appears to others, to be a nice home and car, people will say whatever they feel will put a wedge in a marriage. I had to explain to her how certain individuals will befriend you and yet have their eyes on your spouse.

As to where I am now in my life, I am doing well. I have been through some things but like the old saying goes, "you don't look like what you have been through." Overall, with the support system that I had and the man upstairs, I feel as if I have come out on top. After about twenty years, I was able to have a conversation with my ex-wife and it was at that point that she apologized to me for how she treated me the earlier years. This conversation made me feel better. Then, five years ago, I had to assist my daughter with the burial of her mother.

WORDS OF WISDOM

To the young men of the day, I know we are living in a different era, which I am constantly reminded of this fact by my oldest grandson. He always tells me, "pop it's not like it used to be." Regardless of how it used to be, it still has to be respect. We are not going to always see eye to eye. You have to remember to think and be smart.

If you have a problem, then sit down and try and talk it out. A bone carries a bone. If you can't talk about it, then it's not good. Everything that seems to be against you is not always against you. We are in a different era where the young ladies don't know the true meaning of being a woman and a house woman. No disrespect to anyone. It seems to be all about them. Every time you turn around, they have to get their nails, hair and feet done. How about sitting down and having a family dinner together with a nice hot meal? Those kinds of values I will never forget like the family dinners and gatherings.

Most importantly is to keep people out of your business. Don't try and seek advice from the outside because it's not always what it appears to be. If you need to talk to someone then find someone that has been through it. If you are going to be a man out here today, then be a man. Anybody can make a baby, but it takes a man to see it through until the end. Creating a baby doesn't take long but to be a father goes a long way. It's a lifelong responsibility.

"MOTIVATOR"

GROWING UP

I grew up with both of my parents in the same household and I am their only child. I had a very good childhood. I was able to grow up and watch my parents who were gainfully employed throughout my college years. They provided me with a nice home, to include a home that they purchased in 1975 in a community where there were probably ten Black families in the whole development. They sent me to school. I never went to school or to bed hungry. They made sure I had clothing and some of the things that I wanted, not everything I wanted but most. They were paying for a home, and I wanted a moped which I didn't understand back then. I had no concept when they would say "we don't live in an apartment; we have a mortgage to pay.

I saw love in my home. I didn't come up with fighting in the home or abusive language. It was very evident that my parents loved one another, and that love filtered into the family.

MEMORIES

My most memorable negative moment was when we moved into the home my parents purchased in the '70s. My family was originally living in a city where I was around people who were like me. Upon moving into a different county, I found myself around people who were not like me. I hadn't experienced a lot of racism up to that point in my life. I always remember my mother sharing the story of when I was about nine or ten years of age, and I came home and asked her "what was a n1xxa" because I had never heard the word until we were living in that community. So, that was a big negative memory to me that has always stuck out in my mind.

I also wish that my parents had been more involved in my schooling as far as being active in engaging with the teachers to see where I was heading and what progress I was or was not making. Or even to see what areas I was weak in and needed help. I wish they had been more involved in that aspect.

My most memorable positive moment in my childhood has been when my mother prayed a lot for me. I used to always hear her say my name when she was praying. Even with the love that my parents have for one another, I felt it when I was younger. I not only knew then, but now as I am older, I can still feel the love, what it feels like as well as what it looks like. Knowing that my parents did the best that they could do with the reso0urces they had available to them. I can honestly say that as far as my childhood, I don't have any regrets where I feel as if I missed anything significant. Especially with my father, he was protective of me, where I hung out and who I hung around with. He was very much on top of that.

I went to a couple of elementary schools then completed my high school curriculum in a different school system. After graduating from high school, I was afforded the opportunity to seek out a path for higher education. So, I went forward and attended a community college and then completed law school at a local university.

I am now self-employed, and I own and operate two restaurants and am currently working on a third.

My first daughter was born when I was nineteen and her mother was seventeen years old. We were in a girlfriend/boyfriend relationship at the time. I can definitely say that I was scared. Yes. That was my first emotion. The reason why I was scared was because my mother had told me 'don't ever bring any babies home.' So that stuck in my head. I was afraid to tell her. That stood out more than anything.

After my daughter was born, my relationship with her mom was rocky and tumultuous. We were both very young. When she was born, I was nineteen and a couple of weeks after that I turned twenty. By both of us being so young, we didn't know anything about raising a child. Her mother still being younger than I, wanted to be able to get up and go all the time. This left me in a position to be able to be with our daughter majority of the time. My support system at that time was my parents and my grandparents. It was my family. Being able to get my daughter and keep her for days and weeks at a time wasn't an issue. That was one blessing that my parents provided when I was away in college, they would still get her. They would pick her up, take her home with them and keep her. Especially when she was sick or when an emergency arose. They were the ultimate support system.

I was about thirty-two years old when I married my first wife. My second daughter was from this marital union. Not too long after we married, maybe two years or so, we separated. Co-parenting during this time was tough. A lot of times I felt like I was on the outside looking in. I am sure that my inappropriate actions that occurred at the time more than likely contributed to the reason we were separated.

The result of my actions and behaviors left a very bitter taste in my then wife's mouth. She would even keep our daughter away from my family. This in turn kept our daughter from getting to know my side of the family until she was about six or seven years old. She would come to visit us on occasion but rarely was she able to have overnight visits with me (us). After going through the unnecessary but necessary ups and downs with my daughter's mom, I ended up applying for and receiving full legal and physical custody of our daughter.

Prior to our marriage, my wife had two sons. The fathers of her children were not in the picture so there were no co-parenting issues or outside influences that could have come with being around her children. I always treated her children and raised them as if they were my own biological children. I didn't discriminate between them and my oldest child. However, on a scale of 1-10 with ten being the worst, our marriage along with co-parenting of one another's biological children was probably a four. It had a lot to do with my personality. I didn't try to be daddy. I just tried to be me. I tried to insert the values and my thoughts on how I dealt with them and how I dealt with the situation based on how I was raised. I never spanked them. I just didn't feel like that was my place. So, I guess I just kind of knew my place.

One time the oldest boy was running his mouth while we were in the kitchen, and I pushed him or something. He went back and told his mom, and she came in and got all up in my face and was all mad about that. However, that was the extent of that.

In hindsight, I can now say that one thing that did rub me wrong, for example, if my daughter needed some shoes, I would naturally buy her some. Then my wife would say that the boys should get shoes as well. That was an issue and I remember bringing up the subject and talking to my mom about it on one occasion. I always felt as if they didn't need it, then they didn't need it. It was no different than if my daughter didn't need something, she didn't get it. So that was an ongoing issue between us. It would make me feel as if I were being prodded to have the mindset of you are not going to do for yours without doing for mine.

I am currently married, and we are getting ready to celebrate our fifteenth wedding anniversary. We have one son that has been born of our union. We have a good marriage and it's working fine. The only thing I wish would change is that I feel like she likes to protect him a bit much. I, on the other hand, am a little harder on him because he is a boy. When she gets mad at him, it is open-season, and I can say what I want to him. However, when she is not that mad at him and I go at him, she becomes his protector. Then comes all the over explanations and taking up for him. It could be him not taking the trash out and my wife will provide some type of excuse for his failure to do so.

Overall, it is a great marriage. I have a wonderful wife. One thing is that she is a lot harder on him than I am when it comes to school. I typically think he will eventually get it, where she makes sure he gets it. I do somewhat drop the ball on that part. I do appreciate the initiative that she takes to follow this through, and I make sure that I do tell her so.

My relationship with the mother of my second daughter is much better now. Unfortunately, the mother/daughter relationship for my first daughter has never really been solidified. They never truly bonded as most mothers and daughters do. Even to this day, some of the things that are said or done to my daughter from her mom affects her. My relationship with her is not bad but I do know that I don't joke and play with her as I do with my second daughter's mom. My first daughter's mom has shown that she is unwilling to do what it takes to strengthen their bond and it has impacted our daughters' life even to this day.

Some of the most important things that I feel I have taken from my youth and watching my parents as I became a parent myself are embedded in my life. Being a man and knowing what love looks and feels like and being open minded. The understanding that you are a parent first before you are their friend and being able to balance those two stark situations. For instance, my parents were my parents before they were my friends.

REGRETS

One of my biggest regrets is that I would have liked all my kids to have the same mother. I think about it more than I ever have as I get older. My biggest obstacle in this thought process is to figure out how can I say that to express how I feel to my kids without making them feel anything negative. I don't want them to think that it has anything to do with them per se. It's like when I was practicing law, I used to wonder how I can give up this information without giving up too much just so that person understands where I'm coming from. It is something that I really want them to know this, since they all three have different parents. It's all on me 100%, it's not on them. It is more about how I feel. I just think about how I can say it to them. This is how I feel, or this is how I wish I could have done differently. Not you but as a man and a father what I could have done. As a man, to keep them all together and pouring into them at the same time.

My oldest daughter and my son have been close since day one, but it took a long time and many exercises for both my daughters to become close. That had a lot to do with what was being instilled into my second daughter about my side of the family. However, I made it my mission to see as their father that it happened. I had a lot of guilt behind them not having the same mother. I can truly say at this point that I have succeeded with that. They are all close and I don't treat them any differently. They can always say one is more spoiled than the next but being their father, there is no difference. It was a work in progress though surrounded by a lot of guilt inside of me. To me, as you get older there are some things that you just need to recall, or rethink.

Some of the choices that I have seen my oldest adult daughter make in her life can be cause for concern. However, knowing that she must learn as she lives leaves me to just allow her to do so. It is usually not until she feels the need to speak on certain situations that she may be going through that I give my advice. My second daughter is a lot like me in the way of being more laid back. She takes things in stride and is levelheaded. I feel since my son is the youngest, I am monitoring him a little more with any type of peer pressure he may face. So far things have been easy with him.

WORDS OF WISDOM

When you are a younger parent, don't look at taking care of your child as a task or as a burden. Don't look at the financial piece given to the custodial parent as child support. The custodial parent has a lot of responsibility on them that the non-custodial parent will never know. You have a duty to be the best parent that you can be versus attempting to be the best parent you want to be. They are different. You might want to do something, but you just don't know how to or how to get there or even how to accomplish that.

When I was young, and thinking about the people that I hung around, I was the only one with a child at the time. It restricted me from doing a lot of things that I wanted to do. There are a lot of influences around you. When you are young you have your peers. So, remember that this your duty. These are your marching orders. As you get older you can polish those skills and recognize your mistakes and learn from them. More important, vow not to make those same mistakes again.

In speaking to my brothers, I would like to say this. Stay out of trouble. I tell my son that you can spend five cents getting into trouble and five thousand trying to get out. My father told me if you put your hands in the hands of the white man there is nothing that I can do for you. We as Black men must understand the complexities of the legal system and how it can work for you or really keep you down. All of this plays a part in where you are going in your life.

As far as schooling goes, a job, or as far as how you run a business. It really starts with what you learn and what you see growing up. I didn't see abuse, arguing and all this fighting and destruction. I didn't see any of that. So, I don't carry that baggage with me, but a lot of us do. That goes back to breaking those generational curses.

"Voss Balor"

Growing Up

As I was growing up, it was my mom and three siblings in the household. My dad was active and present in my life. It was just that he and my mom were no longer together as one. There was always a strong presence of adult men in my life. My dad of course, then there were his brothers along with my mom's brothers. They were all a big influence and played their own part in my life. I was blessed to have some good uncles from both sides of the fence as far as learning what to do and not to do as a male. From what I could always tell as I was growing up my parents got along well enough as far as I was concerned and were able to co-parent.

My siblings and I had different fathers. However, my dad was a more prevalent factor in the lives of us all. I was the fourth child in our family composition until two more were added later. In all there were six children but at this point in time two of them have passed.

I had a pretty good childhood growing up. Growing up in the projects, my mom had a good job. I would say that we lived better than the average family. It was evident to us children by being able to take trips to Disneyland and Kings Dominion. We never went without anything and had great Christmases. Our house always looked nice, and we had some good furniture and the way to keep it nice back then was to keep plastic on it. My mom drove a nice Deuce and a Quarter (225, Cadillac).

However, you know as most Black households, you do go through some drama. I mean, as far as seeing your mom go through certain situations with men. For instance, later as my younger brother's father came into play, he was a little rowdier. So, I've seen different things taking place, like the arguing and fighting and things of that nature. I think that's why for me, as a man, I don't particular care for that. I've seen that and went through it as a child growing up. As I got older and became a parent that's something that I was real conscious about. I was not going to do a lot of hoopin' and hollerin' and things around kids. For the most part, I had a pretty good childhood.

As far as my education I did graduate from high school. I did not go to college, but I had already been working and continued to do so. I left the area and went to another state in the South for a little while. I was there for a couple of years and was homesick. So, I returned and have been here ever since. I do kind of regret not going to college now that I have kids who are in college now. Seeing the whole camaraderie with their peers and taking them and getting them settled into their residences at school, makes me wish I had gone myself.

Growing up back in the day in the projects, with a mom that had a pretty good job, and with everything based on your income that made me decide not to go. When I received the paperwork and needed to take it back to my mom, the decision not to jeopardize our housing is what played a part in my thoughts about it and made me not go. In addition, I don't think my mind was wired or helped my mindset on what I was going to do. Now that I am older, I do at times sit back and think about what the four years of college could have done for me, especially seeing my kids doing it. My oldest has already completed her degree and my youngest is working on his master's degree.

As far as my job, I have been employed with them for almost nineteen years. I have been in a managerial position for those years. I do like my job, and I like the people that I come in contact with daily. Keeping with that thought on any job you will always come across times when you feel things can be a little better.

<u>*MEMORIES*</u>

Looking at my childhood, one thing I can say is that I worked pretty hard back in the day. You know back then; a pair of Nike may have been like forty dollars a pair. It was still too much for your parents then, so I had to get me a little job. I used to work at various restaurants washing dishes and doing my homework during that timeframe and then graduating to different positions. Then there were the outside hustles when it snowed. I used to get up early, and shovel snow all day. I could come home with maybe one hundred dollars in my pocket and back then that was a lot of money. I always tried to find my little side hustle and work to have my own money. Overall, I will say I had a pretty good childhood. As I look back now as a grown man, I can't say that I had a bad childhood. Like I said before, we never went without. My mom always provided for all of us.

If I had to pick one negative memory from my childhood, it would be surrounding my mom. I remember seeing her getting stabbed. This was done by somebody she was dealing with. Of course, that was traumatic for me. That changed my perspective as a little boy. It made me commit to never letting anybody do anything to my mom again. That set me on the path of being a protective son, brother, and uncle, to my siblings and the rest of my family. Yes. That was the most traumatic event for me.

You know, when you are young, and you don't understand what's going on and you see the whole aftermath with the ambulance and police and the whole situation. I would definitely say that was my most negative memory of my childhood. So that negative impact on my life helped to pull some positive behaviors out of me that I would be able to use as an adult. To this day, if somebody is out of pocket, (and no I don't go around looking for trouble), then there's business to be dealt with. That's just what it is.

In speaking on the most positive memory as a child that has impacted my life is the core of family. We were always a close-knit family. We were always taking family vacations every year. Whether it was to the country or to the beach or Kings Dominion. I think that's important, and I think even now, my mom instilled this in us up until she left. Your family is your family. I just think that having a really strong family core value is important.

GENERATIONAL TRAITS

Now that I'm a father and I'm dealing with some of the things that I went through with him (my father) I try to always remember to keep my promises to my kids. There were times that he would say, "I'm coming to get you," and you will have your bag packed and he doesn't show up. As a young boy that is kind of hurtful. I mean, overall, my dad was a good man. I don't have anything bad to say about my dad. It's just that those are the little things that you remember from early in your life. When your parent says, "I'm coming to get you on Friday," and you are waiting around, and he is a no show. As a child that made me feel like he doesn't have time for me and leaves me thinking that he could have at least called to say he wasn't going to come through or something. Don't tell me that you are coming, and you don't come. It's always a disappointment when you come across something like that.

However, I do think that the change came from my dad just becoming a better man and a better father and understanding his role a little better. My dad was a hard-working man. He lived in the area and drove for a company for over twenty years. So, the change just came with time and his understanding as a father on what he needed to do. As time went on, our bond was close until the day he left here. It was just more so with him getting better with what he had to do as a father.

My mom did marry again, and it was to my youngest sister's father. He was there for a while. It wasn't a really good time for me because I didn't particularly care for him. I had to deal with that with him, so he wasn't one of my favorite people. As an older person, I respected him but that was about as far as I could get with him. My dislike for him had to deal with not just because he was not my father but more because of how I witnessed how he treated my mom. As time goes on you see different things and you see a person's true colors shine through. So, there was a period when we went through some difficult times with him. At one point, I am a little older and as a young man watching it all unfold, my whole temperament said, "well we can do whatever it is that we need to do." It was times when my oldest sister and I got together and put it on him.

I think there were some instances when my mom may have hidden or sugar-coated things for a lack of a better term, the disrespect she endured from her husband. From what I understand, that's where our last name came from so to maintain the family unit there may have been some excuses made to cover up his poor behaviors. I think they had gotten married early on and then went their separate ways. I can't be one hundred percent sure because I was still fairly young. Then all of a sudden, he pops back up and he is introduced to me as her husband. That's when I asked questions and was told "yes this is where your last name comes from." In hindsight, I do believe there were excuses made to cover up the toxicity that was there.

I am married now and have been like for seven years. We are a blended family with my wife having two biological children and then I have my one. All our kids are grown and out of the house. I don't refer to them as step or bonus kids. When I met her, they were young, and they have been my kids for the last eighteen years. They have been good kids. When I first met them, I told them "I know I'm not your father; but all I ask is that you respect me as who I am." They've always giving me that respect and I love them just as if they were my own kids; just as she does my child. That's always been a good situation.

As far as co-parenting with my non-biological kids' father, I try and let my wife handle that. There of course were times and depending on what it was, she would come and ask me my opinion. At times I would interject but for the most part, I just stayed out of it and let her (them) handle it. It was the same thing with my child when we came together as a blended family. You can correct my child, but it was always the understanding that if at the time when they were young, if somebody needed an *$$ whooping, we would let the appropriate parent do that. Being able to say whatever needed to be said or correct whatever needed to be corrected by either of us has never been an issue in our household.

BECOMING A FATHER

I was thirty-three years old when I learned I was going to be a father. I felt like I was pretty old. My mom would always ask me if I was going to have any kids and I used to say, "nah; I'm good." I always had a ton of nieces and nephews, so I was always content with not having any kids. However, God saw different.

I was in a long-term relationship when I received the news that I was expecting a child. My first emotion was that she had trapped me. Well things within our relationship were raggedy at the time and we were on our way out of it. Then all of a sudden you come up pregnant. This was my first child, so this was something special. As a man you always want a son, but I was blessed with a daughter. The first time I held her, and she looked back at me with her eyes, it has been a wrap ever since.

I have always been in her life, but I can't say that it was not without issues. I have been blessed from the day she was born until now that she has grown up to be a part of her life. I definitely had some issues when she was growing up. I would go home and talk to my mom at times as I went through this journey of being a father and she always told me, "you may not be able to see it right now, but she is not going to be small forever." That has eased me through this process because as I look back now, as time went on, she started to get older. I didn't have to communicate with her mother as much. She would call me and say, "daddy, this is what I need, x y, z." So that would leave her mother and I to be able to communicate on some pertinent things with one another. So, with my daughter aging, it made things much easier for me.

My biggest challenge being a parent is finding out having a son through the blended family versus having a daughter of my own, you must handle girls a lot differently than you do boys. Learning how to approach them differently concerning emotions, feelings, and how you say things. You may not be saying it harshly, but it may be perceived as being that way. Those are some of the things I have learned as time went on. As my daughter has gotten older, we have been able to have conversations and she was able to express herself. She has told me, "well daddy this is how you made me feel at this point in time." With me not having a real understanding or even knowing that its' how I made her feel. Once those talks became more frequent it not only helped her to let me know what was going on, but it helped me to get a better understanding of how my tone along with what I was saying may have sounded to her. So, just being able to communicate and handle feelings differently between the two sexes of children.

I had a great support system. My older siblings were always good aunts and my mom when she was still here. Even my dad gave me support. He loved my daughter, and she loved him. You look at your parents and how they did things when we grew up and see the difference in the relationship between them and your children. My parents were like putty in the kids' hands when they were around. Of course, I noticed it and would always say, "you weren't like that with me!" It was just a little different to see. My daughter would always say, "I'm grandma's favorite." I would of course ask her how she knew that, and her response was always "because grandma told me." My support system was good even until today it's still in effect. Even with her mom's side of things with her people were good. So, my daughter has always had a good village behind her. Even with my wife having hands on her for these last 18 years. When we met, she was small, so my wife has always been a part of her life.

TODAY IN SOCIETY

Now that she is older and with the prominence of life with the internet and BBLs, people altering themselves and all that comes with it, these are the type of conversations that I have had and continue to have with my child. I explain to her that God made you who you are. I give her my opinion on how I feel about things and then I remain mindful of what and how I say to her. Any type of influence is more prevalent now than when she was younger. As harsh and as crazy as things are now, with social media and kids wanting to be somebody that they are not. I try to remind her that she is who she is. God made you as you are so just go with that. If you are born with a pudgy nose, there's no need to have surgery to fix it. Just go with it as it is. I have heard her say things about wishing she could change this or that. At this point, even though she is an adult, I still must be mindful of how she is thinking and how she is feeling about certain things. I just try to be positive and let her know you are who you are and don't let anyone make you feel as if you need to be someone other than who you are.

REGRETS

I really don't have any regrets as to how I have approached parenthood. I feel as if I have always been a good father. I just wish that I had a better understanding about this early on. Some things that I allowed and went for now that I know would have been different. I definitely would not have put up with some things just so that I could see my child. The times when you feel you are not allowed to see your child because they are being used as a pawn or as leverage in an argument. I did allow some of those to happen because I of course wanted to see my child. However, if I were able to turn back the hands of time, I definitely wouldn't be going for some things that I went for.

One thing that I always tell my daughter to this day is for her to sit back and look over her life. There has never been a time when you were without or didn't have what you wanted. I don't think there is anything that I would change but only to have a better understanding of being a parent and dealing with a scorned woman and how that level of drama can unfold. This was all new to me, so I'm learning on the fly and dealing with all kinds of issues. Regrets for real? No.

WORDS OF WISDOM

I know at this point in time that you are probably going through a tough situation with the child's mother or whatever the situation may be, just keep plugging at it. There is no book on being a father. I think that you as a man you will have to want to be in your child's life. Don't ever let anyone take that from you or not allow you to be a part of your child's life. It's going to be some tough and trying times. It's going to be some days when you ask yourself if it's all worth it. You have to understand that you should never slight your child because of something else that somebody else has done to you. It's not the child's fault.

So, you as a father have a job to raise and nurture them as you are supposed to. You just have to fight the fight. It's not going to be easy, but you as a man and as a father, you have to fight the fight for your child. It will pay off in the long run. Sometimes when you only hear one side of the story, you tend to believe that side of the story. As the saying goes, there are three sides to every story. My side, your side, and the truth. Just don't give up. As a man you are built to endure and overcome everything that you're dealing with for your child or children. Just stay fast my brother and hang in there because it's gonna get better. You may not be able to see it right now, but trust me, it gets better.

"Brandon X"

Growing Up

I had a great childhood. One of the things about people my age, we spent a lot of time outside. Everybody had kids in the neighborhood, and we played from sunup until sundown and right before the lights came on, we had to come home. I didn't think that when I was growing up but as I got older, I thought back on what it was like. I really did have a great childhood.

I did not know that I was poor. We lived in a rooming house, and I just thought that was normal until we moved into the projects when I was twelve years old.

I didn't have both parents in the household. I had just my mom and of course the other people that lived in the house. They were just like other parents. They took care of me; they loved me and even disciplined me when it was necessary. The whole neighborhood was like that. It's just how it was growing up in an urban area across the street from a popular carryout place where everyone frequented and the ladies that cooked the food could really cook. Those were the good days.

I have only one big brother. He went away to the service when I was six years old. That was a lonely time for me because I missed him so very much. Even though he was always in the streets, I just knew he was there. I did miss him when he was gone. When he came home, I was of course outside playing about a half a block away from the house. I looked up and he was standing on the corner watching. That was a happy day for me. He is twelve years older than I, so we really didn't have an association outside of the house. He did take me places and introduced me to things like during the Sonny Liston and Cassius Clay (Muhammad Ali) fight they had for the world championship. He took me with him to watch the fight. That was an experience right there that I will never forget.

My brother and I have different fathers. My brother's father was from the deep South. That is where my brother was born. My mom's family moved to another state, but my mom decided to move to the state I grew up in. My dad lived in the City. He was in the area and a part of my life. My uncle who lived a block away from us was a big influence on my life as I was growing up as well. In addition to him, my best friend's dad was another male influence in my life. They were both dynamic male influences in my life. I learned how to be a parent from them. I saw the good and the bad.

I attended school in the area and when I finished high school, I went to college. I attended college for a few semesters, eventually deciding to do a couple of trade schools in electronics and real estate.

MEMORIES

It is very difficult to think of a negative memory surrounding my mom because she did everything. Although I will say that the biggest negative thing was when they would whip our butts back then. If somebody did that today, they would go to jail. However, back then my most memorable negative was my fault. I was going to run away because she wouldn't let me go to the movies. I had packed my little bag. I packed everything up but food. She let me do all of that, pack my bag, sit on the steps, and pout. Then when it was time to get in bed, I got in the bed and went to sleep. Boyyy!!! She woke me up with the first lick and then I snatched the belt out of her hand. When she got it back, the buckle was facing me and never stopped. That's the only negative I can remember about my mom. That right there changed my whole direction. I was a defiant child.

I want to add this little story. This is how defiant I was. We were at church, and they had this little snack bar where they sold candy and chips. I was crazy about Baby Ruth, and I wanted one. Me not knowing that she didn't have any money, I wanted it. She told me not to touch it. I touched it anyway. I picked it up. Then she told me to put it back. I didn't. I opened it. Then I took a bite. When I found myself again, I was on the other side of the room. Oh, but guess what? I had that candy bar. I ate that candy bar. It was worth finding myself on the other side of the room.

She broke me out of that behavior. She broke me out of it with that belt buckle. That was the day she turned my life around. I still have a little dent on my head as a reminder.

As far as my dad goes. My only negative thing I can think of is that he would never come to any of the programs that were being held at school and everyone else's parents were there and mine wasn't. I don't know if it had any type of impact on my life or not. I really can't say. I wasn't conscious of it if it did. I didn't hold it against him. It wasn't too much I held against him. I didn't even hold it against him that he wasn't there all the time because my mom made sure she was there enough to fill in all the gaps. What my mom put in superseded what my dad did not.

One thing my mom did was she raised both my brother and I like men. It was no feeling sorry. There was tough love when we needed it. We were told to channel our emotions inside. We were told to stop crying. Did I cry? Yeah, I cried. Did I cry long? Yeah, I cried for a minute. A lot of times when I got hurt, I didn't cry because I already knew that I wasn't going to get any sympathy for it. There were many times I got hurt playing and I know I needed to go to the hospital. But did we go? No. She grabbed some salve (an ointment used to promote healing from skin wounds), slapped it in the hole and sent me back outside.

BECOMING A FATHER

 My first child, and oldest daughter was born when I was fifteen years old. Did I know how to be a father? No, but I tried the best I could. During the early years of me feeling life and parenting out, my mom was my biggest supporter. In addition, my daughters' grandmother also stepped in quite a bit to help and support as well.

Her mom tried to keep me away from her. During this time, I got married at the age of twenty-two and from that marriage was birthed a son and a daughter. However, eventually my oldest daughter's mother gave her to me. So, I had custody of my daughter along with my wife at the time. This happened when she was about to turn fifteen years old. Once my daughter moved in, our communication was bad because she was going through her rebellious stage. That was the reason her mom handed over the reins to me. So, it was a work in progress in even getting to the point where we could communicate with one another. This was definitely a trying time, and we were always in each other's face, because due to the age difference we were just like brother and sister.

My daughter had always been in/out of the household prior to me obtaining custody. She was always there because I was her dad. She was there during summer breaks from school, holidays and more. From that point on she was in my household until she got married and for a short time afterward.

Both my wife and I had a part in ensuring that our family and home life ran as smooth as possible. One thing we did was to make sure that the kids were involved in sports at a very young age. So that was our life. That was our dynamic and we did that together. I did the coaching, and she was the team mother. Not only did we blend our family, but we blended other people's families with ours because the other kids on the team mostly hung out with us all the time. Most of the time their parents didn't have to do anything. We would have them with us so we had to feed them, and we would get them home in time for them to go to bed after practice or a game.

Over the years of my marriage, my wife and I opted to be foster parents to over forty children that came through the foster care system. There were many different situations that we found ourselves intertwined in while coaching at our old basketball program. We had a lot of kids that came through there that needed help. We had five teams, so we saw many different kids and my wife worked with a municipal program, so she saw a bunch of different situations. So, when we were asked would we become involved, we agreed because we did see the need for foster parents in the area. We fostered children for about four years before we ended up adopting two boys. We were the poster board for the foster care system. There was a training video that was used featuring my wife and I and the first two children we adopted. The video was used to show all the foster care parents around the country. Once we adopted the first two, that took us out of the foster care pool. We were removed from the pool at that point because we had more than the allotted number of participants within one household. However, later down the road we ended up adopting a daughter, that we at one time had as a foster child, who was a teenager at the time.

Coming from fostering to adopting these children had allowed us to create bonds filled with love, respect, and permanency. There are no differences in standards, rules and morals taught or expected from our biological or adopted children. That's how relationships are taught within the family unit. We have our ups and downs and our highs and lows. We were very fortunate with our biological children and with the three adopted children.

I have a fiancé' and we have been together for about ten years now. She came into our relationship with an adult son as well as a minor daughter. Although the term stepson/daughter is what is used to describe children from blended families, everyone is a whole within our unit. So, in speaking of my stepdaughter, she was a teenager when I came into her life. There had been no previous contact with her biological father, therefore, I was able to pick up the torch and lead the way for her as well.

When I started dating my fiancé' her son was an adult already. He is twelve years the senior of his sister. Yet I still to this day sit down with him, have talks to try and guide and lead him. I have never had to per se discipline my stepdaughter, but I have had to have a talk with her about things. My fiancé' has also had to talk to mine surrounding disciplinary issues or when things are going or about to go awry. Even as adult children, certain conversations may come into play when we as the parents see that things may need to be addressed. Just as with my biological and adopted children, they receive all the love and guidance as with the others.

The most challenging issues I may have had was when I was a new parent. As a young parent I found myself doing things out in the streets that made me stop and think about things differently. I also had to stop and think about my child, and it made me change my course. At times things could have gone another way but I was thankful that I was able to have her to grasp onto. I had to understand that this was not the way that I want to go in or with my life. Overall, my focus has always been on my kids. That's the way it was until my wife of thirty-five years passed away and then I kind of flaked out for a little while. It was then that my fiancé' helped me tremendously to get back to my reality. I sacrificed all of what I ever wanted to do to make sure that they were good from day one.

WORDS OF WISDOM

As a father one of the main things that you can adapt to your way of life and your thought process is patience. You can have all the love that you can muster up for your child but if you lack patience then it will put you in a place where you may be overwhelmed. Remember to always reach out and ask for help. If you don't have a father of your own, reach out to a relative or an experienced father that you know. Always speak up for your family. You will find in your walk the difference between argumentative and being an advocate. Use each way wisely. If something doesn't feel right or you have a gut feeling, then by all means follow that feeling for it is the gut that communicates with your brain. In everything you do, make sure it is done out of love and never spite. Your walk, the way you respect others, and the way you love comes out through your children.

GROWING UP

I grew up in a household with both of my parents present. They have been married for fifty-two years. I am the only child of their union. Their one and only heir to the throne. Most people automatically think of the words "brat" or even "spoiled" when they find out that I have no siblings. However, we are West Indians, and my father absolutely did not believe in that. He is a firm believer in hard work. I have been working since the age of eleven.

It was from his upbringing that he knew what he knew. Therefore, he instilled it all into me from the very beginning. I have always told people that he raised me out of fear instead of development because it was a nice mix, but it was more fear than development. As most Black men that were raised back in the '60's and '70's, I was more afraid than I was anything because I was really learning while I was doing things.

I would say that I had a great childhood. As far as discipline, my father was the disciplinarian of the household. However, my mom was in charge of the developmental pieces of my life.

MEMORIES

My father cheated a lot. He would take me on the weekends just around with him running his errands and other stuff. We would go to these two ladies' house. One of them happened to be a coworker and the other was a party of his Army Reserve unit. It was cool. I would run around and play with the kids and naturally I didn't think anything of it. My father being the dude that he was, used to have this work bag and he would always tell me, "don't go in my work bag, don't mess with that bag."

However, I was a latchkey kid. So, when they are gone, I am at home by myself. It was a weekend, they had left, and I was of course, by myself. I see the bag and think to myself, "hmmmm, I wonder why he keeps telling me not to go into this bag?" Of course, I go in the bag, and I see a naked picture of one of the ladies. Fast forward and one day, I get into trouble. Something had happened and I told a lie about it, and he confronted me about it. My father tells me that I am one of the most dishonest people I have ever met. Mind you, this is my father talking to his child. So, I said to him, "oh really?" I go grab the picture and bring it out on the table and say to him "so if I'm dishonest then what is this?" That undoubtedly created a big tiff between myself, my mother, and my father. My mom rolled out, left for a while. She went back to the Caribbean; she went to the islands for like six months. She got herself together and came back with her agenda of what's happening and what's not happening, and he snapped to it, and he has been right ever since. I did some crazy stuff, and he did some crazy stuff but that was how I found out what it was. That was the most memorable negative moment in my childhood that sticks out to me.

I have a lot of positive memories. I have been fortunate to travel extensively. I have been all over with them. It's also been good to see them proud of my academic and sports accolades. I can truly say that I have better than bad memories. Just like major milestones I played sports, so I did well, just as academically I did well.

My educational background consists of graduating from the only high school in the City and an HBCU in the same state. I obtained a degree in Psychology/Sociology. I am in juvenile corrections and have been in this field for 26 years.

I am currently looking at working two more years then I will be retiring.

I found out that I was going to be a father when I was twenty-four years old. I was in a long distance, committed relationship that was supposed to be exclusive. However, I was not exclusive where I was living. I was happy when I found out though. I was ready. So, it was my excuse to slow down, which is a bit weird, but I realized I was about to have a baby, so you better slow things down for your daughter. That's it.

I was afraid because I wasn't a grown up. I was still trying to be a kid, trying to run the streets. I thought I was cool, and I was trying to be a player. Then all of a sudden, now, you have to get a career. It's time to be locked in and focused. I am looking at my parents thinking how I have to worry about a household. I have to provide things for school and worry about my benefits. So, then that had me worrying about different benefits at a job. I also had to start thinking about where I was going to live and the change in the things that I wouldn't be able to buy for myself anymore. I had to understand how I couldn't buy certain shoes anymore and if you know me, then you know that was "the real" that hit me.

My daughter's mother and I decided to remain long distance in our relationship. However, I would travel every other week, so I was there a lot. Of course, it was pre-Zoom and other types of video calling. Without those pieces of technology and my determination to be an ever-present dad I was always on the road, ensuring that I saw her. I made sure that my daughter always understood that I didn't live right around the corner to eliminate any disparities she may have to deal with at any given time thinking that I did not want to be involved or was not concerned about her.

I have always remained a constant in her life from the beginning. From sending letters, postcards, Hallmark cards, trinkets, or something. I wanted to always let her know that she was on my mind, in my heart and that I loved her. Anytime she did something in school, or just because, I may call the school on any given day and have the office call her to the office informing her that she has a phone call. She would then come to the office, and I would be on the other end of the line telling her that I just wanted to say hello and want you to have a good day at school. I stayed committed to that. I made sure to give her everything that I didn't get growing up. I was determined to give her everything that my father did not give me developmentally and then some and I still do.

Her mom and I have always had a great level of communication between us. We never had an adverse relationship. We have never had beef. It's just been the distance. We both have been long term at our places of employment, respectively. We tried to figure it out by looking at the two different jobs and making a way. She would call though and keep me well informed of everything our daughter was going through, good, bad, or indifferent. Whatever she felt as though I could get a better point across or provide a different point of view to, she would ask me to talk with her about it and I would oblige. It could be about anything. Let's say boys. Well, I am not going to talk to her about boys on the phone. I am going to drive down and handle it. We have a very good relationship with one another.

At this point in my life, I am not involved with my daughter's mother. I am not involved with anyone. However, we are on track. She and I are doing our thing, long distance but I am not involved in anything here at home, but I am exclusive to her. So outside of that, I am just working in corrections along with my other professional gigs. I just continue to go down there and check on them on the weekends.

My daughter is eighteen years old and in college now. She is doing very well in school. She was on campus and didn't really like it there. So, I bought a home down there nearby for her and her mom and I had her move from off campus. My thoughts at that time were why pay money for a dorm when you have a home close to school. She can now stay at home, save her money, and go to school. Now she has been able to secure a work study job along with two other jobs in addition to going to school.

GENERATIONAL TRAITS

I took that fear piece, as I'm older and I understood where he (my father) was coming from. True story. My daughter and her good friend are going on a trip down South to visit this dude who is in the military that she is currently dating. I'm thinking, he is a good, upstanding young dude in the military, and he can be held accountable if something goes on. My thoughts about this are the way things are now, there are two young Black girls driving. So that's my thing, instead of me going hard on her about "don't do this" or "don't do that," I just advise her to be careful when you go down there, fill your gas tank up during the day and make sure you are watching your surroundings.

So, instead of cussing at her and scaring her about going there and driving, I'm just giving her developmental ways of how to handle things. I want her to go and be happy that you are doing these things, but realistically this is what I am afraid of. That's what I took from my father. Just giving her the real. Then my mother with the nurturing side of it. I want you to explore, I want you to be eighteen and a woman. However, these are the things that I want you to be aware of. I know they are going to do what they want to do, and it won't be because she doesn't know. It's going to be because she is being just whatever she is being. I have just tried to take all the negative traits from my father and turn them into a positive. Take the nurturing side from my mom and just mix them all together.

I have to always remember back when my father said, "don't go in the bag," I wasn't even thinking about it at the time. It wasn't until he said something about it that made me wonder why he was saying it and I wanted to know what was in it. So, I am clearly not going to tell her not to go on the trip. I am in another state and have no way of knowing that she is going after I have told her not to. So, instead of opening the door for that type of situation, I just try to prepare her for what it is that I know she wants to do.

I just want to make sure that my daughter is overall fully aware of anything that she may have to deal with. When I was in school, one of my coaches pulled me to the side and asked me if I was having sex. Later, the question came from my mom. That conversation was more sensitive, but it was also to explain to me how to be a gentleman and what a woman would like. It's the things that you say and the things that you do. Just as with other conversations that I have had with my daughter and ensuring that she was comfortable with being able to handle herself when it comes to the possibility of an intimate relationship with boys. I am not playing any games with this situation. Slick has been slicking a long time. She will never be able to say she wasn't schooled, told nor informed about anything that I as her father already had knowledge of.

The only tribulation that I have had with being a parent is not being able to be there with her daily. It bothers me because I want to be able to tuck her in and hold her when she comes home from having a bad day. I don't want the phone call; I want to be there. I want to be able to give her the space in her room and then allow her to come to my room and sit on my bed and have a conversation with me. I want to be able to physically be there to console her. Not say anything, just listen to her. That also goes for the good stuff. Be there for her when she is smiling and laughing. The two of us have our own handshake, we're funny. So yes, my tribulation is not being there physically.

REGRETS

I don't have any type of regrets at all. When it clicked in, I immediately said, "I got this." I don't believe in regrets. God blessed me. He gives you your famine, He gives you your test and you see how you are going to work it and you keep it moving. So, He gave me my test and I passed it. I have a child; I gotta go.

TODAY IN SOCIETY

Fortunately, my daughter does not do a lot of social media outlets. I have told her to stay off that. So, she does have a very small account that she will be on Snap Chat for a second, but that stuff comes and goes. As far as it is defining her, and who she is, I have made sure she knows who she is, so she isn't going to do it. Her peer influences are okay, it's all right. At one point she was hanging out with a group that wasn't as cool.

Let me tell you how good God is. She was hanging with a group of people, smoking weed, it's not a problem. I've told her that I have seen a lot of crime scene photos of youngins, who were fifteen and sixteen slumped over in cars, where they have been into something and the girl who was with them was innocent. She is getting ready to go to college but she's in the car with them and they are getting ready to come and kill her because she's in the car with a dude who isn't about nothing.

So, lo' and behold this guy she was dating, he was killed the same way, in a car. He had just dropped her off and then he drove somewhere else. He pulled over and stopped somewhere else and the guys rolled up on him and killed him. That's what I tell her always. Be careful and be mindful of who you hang around with and what they are doing because you never know. Yes, her peer pressure was crazy at one point, but she did get it back on track. So, now she is solo. This one girl she is going on a trip with, that's all she travels with. That's it. In hindsight, it hasn't really been that bad. So, things are not bad because with her self-identification, she is good with that.

MY FEARS

The red flag for me that I have paid attention to is the conduct and how they talk to her. I look out for the type of communication i.e., whether they DM her through her social media or do they talk on the phone. I also look out for whether he talks about sex off the break, or is he a smoker, a drug dealer, a deviant, or a hood dude. I also look and inquire about his background. I check to see if he wants to meet me, does he have a relationship with his father. So, boys without fathers, then I say to myself "let me tap in a little bit" to get a better understanding of who they are and where their head is.

Of course, on a sexual tip I did some weird stuff growing up. I have remembered that things don't change too much. I want to make sure she is clear in understanding that the fellas are going to come at her with different propositions that could lead to having sex. I prepare her for the multitude of explanations that she could receive from a guy who does not want to protect himself within an intimate situation. I have even made sure to school her on checking out her environment when she visits someone's home. I tell her to look behind doors, in bathrooms, check out the closets and more because there could be someone hiding somewhere waiting either for "their turn" or to secretly watch or video. Especially since everything is via social media and the internet. You just never know who may be trying to set you up. If he is against you checking out the place to make you feel more comfortable with the situation, then you roll out. I have to say, when I was young, I was a dude in the closet while my man was having sex with a girl, or I was somewhere in the house laid back and not watching but still there.

I have told her to be mindful of all that stuff. All the tricks of the trade. I don't care how cute he is. None of that.

DO OVERS

I do not have anything that I would do over. My mother sat me down and told me, "son, give your absolute best." I have done that....given my absolute best day.

WORDS OF WISDOM

I would tell another young man that life is going to come at you fast. You are going to have to learn how to be responsible. The baby will make you be responsible or like my father used to say, "it might cost you a little; or might cost you a lot; but it's going to cost you." Seek out real men. Go talk to someone. You may be in school, and you see a teacher and think to yourself that he exemplifies something that I like in a man. I really need to talk to Mr. Johnson about how he rolls, or I need to talk to my coach about this or whomever, a janitor may be a solid dude. You can always go to someone responsible and say, "hey man I'm having a baby and I need some advice."

Just really seek out some good mentors that can really give you guidance and structure as it pertains to these kids. I wish I had that when I was younger. To have an older guy or a guy that was seasoned and worthy to give me that conversation. Not just a dude, but a worthy cat that could give me that information. A cheat sheet to life so that you don't make those turns that those before you made. You don't have to go the same way because we've done this already and it didn't work out well. If you are in school, try and stay in school, get some employment, and hopefully get your parents involved. Get you a good solid base with the mother of your child. Even when you are meeting and dating people you are not thinking about the long haul. Like I tell my daughter, when you are dating someone and slip up you end up dating him, the family and everybody's involved. So, if you end up with all these individual clowns, you end up with a whole bunch of clowns to deal with on that side of the coin. Just try to be responsible and tighten up and find some people that can really give you the guidance that you need to succeed.

"OMAR SWANSON"

Growing up as an only child was challenging. I was in need of so much companionship, such as a sibling and a father figure I could look up to and teach me the ins and outs of transitioning from a boy to a man. My mother was a struggling single parent and was unable to provide the lifestyle I thought I deserved as a child. I used to feel really lonely and confused as to why I didn't have certain materialistic things and why my father was seldom around. I used to wonder why I would teach myself everything. I had to really adapt and learn about my environment and people by myself. I really needed some guidance.

My father was not around. He would come through like once a month. When he did stop by to interact with me, it was usually negative. I remember only seeing him when I used to get in trouble at school. That would be our relationship...him coming through just when I was in trouble or when it was some type of issue.

My dad never showed up just to show love or just to show his face or show up with gifts. Even once I went to live with him, he was always at work. Even when he wasn't at work he would never communicate. He was just unavailable. We never hung out and he barely even engaged with me. He would not even make the effort. Made me feel like I wasn't even worth the attention or love.

EMOTIONAL RESIDUE

My feelings about my relationship with my dad left a negative impact on me as I was growing up. I had to do other things. I looked more at my friends for wisdom, knowledge, and guidance. He did little to no teaching me on how to be a man, I mostly grew up when I was in jail. I got around older gentlemen that taught me things. You know that all people that are locked up are not all bad people. I gained more knowledge from the older guys who were in jail and who really went through some things and lost some things. They really gave me some sound advice on how to really be a man at that time.

MEMORIES

My most positive experience from my mom was when she taught me how to drive. I was so scared to make a left turn at this certain main intersection by my apartment complex and she said to me "Nope! Not this time. I'm not touching the wheel. You can do it." That's one of the first times I remember overcoming a fear and obstacle. That was a life lesson to never let fear and doubt stop me from where I'm going in life.

My worst experience with my mom was at one point when my son's mother alienated me from interacting with my son and my mom was seeing him and not informing me. During that time period, her and I interactions slowed down for like a year or so.

With my dad I have many negative memories. I guess the ultimate one was when I tore my ACL playing blacktop basketball. I worked hard to get a basketball scholarship and into the U.S. Navy. One week before training camp I tore my ACL and he actually believed that I did something to purposely tear my ACL. He is such an egotistical person, even thinking about him at times I get so mad. Like why would I tear my ACL on purpose?

My best experience with my dad was when he got me a car. I was in high school, and I made the president's list. My name was even in the paper. So, I was asking my dad to buy me a car at the time. I wanted a Caprice and at that time they were like fifteen hundred to two thousand dollars. He went and bought me a 2002 Honda Accord. That was my best experience I would say.

As a young boy, pre-teen or teenager, my relationship with my dad left me unprepared for life. For the most part, I learned everything on my own. At that time in my life, I still didn't know anything. I started reading everything when I was in my mid 20's. Before then I was just deaf, dumb, and blind listening to what everybody else was talking about. Watching TV, going off of he-say, she-say and not relying on facts. I was pretty lost for a long period of time because I wasn't basing my life on facts. So, I wasn't prepared, and I feel like a lot of things that I should have learned, experienced or been educated about, I learned late.

Back when I was growing up we didn't have social media and the internet wasn't like this information era it is now. So now I'm in an information era I'm a little distraught. Had it been like this when I was growing up, I would have been alright. I would have been good. Even without my dad's help or guidance I would have been able to figure things out with the help of the internet. I feel like I have come to my epiphany like "oh wow, but I'm damn near 40". No matter where I go, people act as though they are terrified. They look like "God almighty!" That's just my everyday life from being 6'7", dark skin, and with locs.

After graduating high school with a 3.5 GPA, I enrolled into community college to be a radiologist but later I dropped out because my son was born, and I then became a full-time dad. I then went toward a different path and obtained my real estate license. Later, I moved to down South and went to school for Entrepreneurship and Small Business Management. I did like a year there and completed the course. Upon completion I went to a university for barbering where I obtained my barber hours. I am very comfortable with the career that I have. I thank God that I can take care of myself, my mom, and kids. It was one of the best decisions I ever made because I got into the program for free being a D.C. resident at the time and I was just coming out of jail. I was cutting hair in jail, but I still didn't know if I wanted to take it seriously or whatnot because I was still transitioning from becoming a boy to a man mentally.

So now I have been cutting hair for the past almost two years consistently. It's the first time I feel like I have been stable in my life. I don't have to rely on selling drugs or weed to survive or "work a job." It's been really fulfilling for me and rewarding. I take it very seriously and it's just a passion of mine now. It also helps me deal with a lot of emotional things on a day-to-day basis. Like when I am working on someone for thirty minutes on a haircut, that's time I am focused on them and helping someone else other than myself. It allows me to take my eyes off my own issues.

BECOMING A FATHER

I was about twenty-three years old and in a relationship with my girlfriend when I found out I was going to be a father. I am more of a monogamous person. I don't deal with too many women so of course it was someone I was dealing with for an extended period of time. She just told me that she was pregnant. I remember I was excited because it was my first child. Abortion was a topic that she talked to me about, but

I was against it because growing up in church I felt and believed that it was murder. I told her that if she did move forward with the termination then I would get a tattoo of a teardrop on my eye symbolizing murder.

Me moving into the role of being a dad was pretty easy. I just show genuine love, concern, and patience. Being a father is super easy. I just don't understand how men don't do it! The lack or what my father didn't do with me is the opposite of what I do with my kids. It's just too easy, too simple. For a "man" over the age of twenty-one, to grow up in a house without their father, then to have a son and not know what to do, is jive-like dumb. Being a dad just takes patience. I have that. I'm not going to fake it like when I had my kids. Even with my stepdaughter and raising her at the time, I looked at her as my own. I have unlimited patience with the kids. They are mine. I brought them here and no one else is going to give them information, or the love or the genuine truth like me. I mean someone else may give them the general truth and stuff about life but nobody's going to love them like me. I don't think any other man on this planet can love my son more or my daughter more than I. He or She may come close but that would be a different type of love.

Going back to my stepdaughter, when I met her mom, she was already born, and they were struggling. I wanted to help her out. I got into a relationship with her mom. I was just trying to be a helpmate in a sense because she was working, had a daughter, and she didn't have a man. I wanted to kind of be there for her. You know I'm just one of those types of guys. I want to add value to where I'm at. So, if I'm not needed or valued, I don't even want to be around.

My relationship with my stepdaughter was awesome. Right now, it's in shambles. She did not know I wasn't her real father because I was there since she was two years old. During me and my ex's breakup I guess she told her that I wasn't her real father. Now it's just a different energy when I come around. It's just completely thrown off and I hate it.

Now I tread lightly with our relationship because that really hurt me. I don't wanna go through that again. I don't want to get so close, and I get hurt like that again. I still look at her as my daughter, but I can't even call her phone now because of the disconnect that me and her mom have. I feel like that was a bond and a relationship that was so pure and genuine because my stepdaughter looked at me as her dad. She honestly thought I was her dad. Even on her birthdays she was always asking 'where's my daddy.' The party wouldn't even be a party without her daddy. So now, I keep from trying to get left out in the cold by giving people my all. That really hurt me and still hurts me to this day. That's something that I deal with every day with her and my own daughter.

In addition to my stepdaughter, I have my son and a daughter who all share the same mother. We were in a relationship with one another for a good time frame and then we split up. When we split it up there was no real question of 'what are we doing.' It was just as if we were mad at each other or something like that. Years went by and she and I got back into the relationship only to realize this isn't what I wanted. You know you expect people to change over the years. You know, get better or be already working on themselves. Speaking of me. The amount of work that I put into myself and the expectations I have for myself is astronomical compared to others. So, when I got back with her, I thought that she might have gone through this growth spurt. Like a maturity thing or even a level up mentality. That was a disconnect. That's why when I got back with her in the sense, I really got back with her just to be in my kids' life because I wasn't around for so long that I was just trying to make up for lost time. I ended up just settling for less just to be with the kids.

Not taking away from my parents and their parenting of me, I would say that my father instilled discipline and my mom just gave genuine love. These are skills that I use in my parenting. I feel like if you want to be a good parent you must read. You must take the time out to educate yourself and apply it. Not just read it and don't apply it. Or read it and don't understand it. I look at myself as being my own man and know that I had to break the generational curse of "lack" and "want." Of not taking the time out to be better or the time out to gain the knowledge on how to be better. Playing with people's mental state; a child's mental state. Like the mother of my child is playing with the child's mental state and it is affecting other people's well-being. I really don't go off my parent's philosophy too much. Their philosophy to me is more so on religion. I feel like my parents' era or age, everything was more about labor, work and religion. In this era, they are not really promoting that. They are not really promoting work, it's entrepreneurship. Different time, different stuff. Religion is not a big thing nowadays. It is more entertainment to me. Stuff is just getting so different. People are adapting with change.

At this point, I don't have any type of relationship with the mother of my children. As far as being able to co-parent, that is non-existent. On her part, she comes from a place of control. I have noticed that the majority of masculine and over emotional women of color tend to be very controlling and entitled. Not having a good relationship with my children's' mother affects every aspect of my life. It's a big deal. We have no communication at all. To be honest, I prefer that. I just don't want to not be in my children's' lives. I feel like there isn't a need for me to talk to her anyway.

Unless it is about the kids or an emergency. My stance in reference to that is that I would rather have no communication with you period. No association. Just because she is the type of person to keep her kids away from their father. I'm honest with myself and I will say there is no legitimate reason. It's crazy.

I don't get to communicate with my children regularly. I do get to talk to my son. I don't get to talk to my daughter of course because she is too young and only two years old. My son and I talk daily. I reach out to him every day. My personal feelings are I feel like we have lost our connection. Well, we do have a connection but it's just not as strong as I would like it to be. I feel like me not being in his life daily or being around my energy to see what a man is all about and to see why women are completely different from us. I feel like that's important to know but also understand. I don't really get to see him as much and I don't really get to talk to him as much. Now that he's getting older, I'm not saying he is more distant, but he is growing up. He wants to do more things on his own. So, I don't get to interact with my kids on a daily or consistent basis. I also absolutely do not have any say in his educational plan. I just honestly feel like Black men, don't have any say so in anything that matters. Like their children and even their finances. I just feel like I don't have much of a word. My word as a man doesn't hold any weight. As they say, men's feelings don't really matter. We are supposed to toughen it up.

This as a man makes you feel belittled and unappreciated. I am just looked at as a source of money or a source of income. No one is going to ever give me anything. Ever. Not that I'm even looking for it because I don't even know what that is because no one gives me anything. I've always said that. I told my mom that.

It's just been me. So, I guess like I said, I am just looked at as a source of income or like when people are lacking, they come and holler at me. It's like gimme, gimme, gimme all the time and no one wants to invest in me. I just feel like it's more so just expectations. Like I don't expect anything from anybody, but people always expect so much from me. I don't want the kids or people to just want my money. Yet I am supposed to act or conduct myself in a certain way and I'm supposed to give off a certain energy every day, always. I just feel like I don't get treated like a human being, I get treated more like a robot because no one really cares about me or about what I must do or nothing. No one really cares and it's cool, I've accepted that. For a man and his feelings, his time, his money, his wants, his needs. Like I've said before, everything in my life that I've experienced, I was shocked to know that it stings. However, if I never got shocked, I would have never gotten to know that it stings because no one is ever going to take the time out to tell me 'Hey this stings' or 'you know if you go over there, it's going to sting.'

If I had the opportunity to have my children full-time as opposed to the way things are now, I wouldn't do anything differently as a parent. I would still make the effort to instill in them what I do now. Love is T.I.M.E. Just waking up and getting a hug from your child. Or just waking up and seeing your kid in the refrigerator. Or just waking up and them asking me a question and me giving them an honest answer or the best answer that I know as a father. That's what life's about. You know that feeling for me to give them my guidance to my children. I'd say more so that I would be doing something different with them and that's reading. I'm big on reading. So, every day we would set up an hour for reading because that is important.

If I were running my own household, if I had full control

over my household, with my woman and stuff like that, things would be different. That's one thing that I would do because I feel it's very important. Certain days of course I would have game night. It's more of creating that bond and teaching these kids to try and think for themselves. That would be my most important thing and taking time to read to them every day showing them that it's important. Reading every day will create a habit for them because we are slaves to our habits whether they are good or bad. I would also go throughout the week by setting up something that we would do every day because education begins at home. I would just set up more interactive things for us to do. Hence social media or them being on their phones. I would have to be over the top with it to let them know that I am purposely doing this to and for y'all. I don't want them to get caught up in the "scroll" of social media. I would include some basic life skill teachings of how to communicate effectively with people. I would also ensure I show them how to eat right, exercise daily and make sure they know how to use their time wisely. God gave us twenty-four hours a day and if you sleep nine or ten hours a day, what are you going to do with the remainder of that time? It's about teaching my son how to be a man, because I don't know how to be a woman.

TODAY IN SOCIETY

Since I am not there daily to have an impact on everything, I do believe that society plays a significant role in influencing the upbringing of my son. I feel that a father should be in his son's life daily. As an American who else can positively influence and teach my son how to conduct himself around others who are not like him. When they see us as tall, dark skin with locs, and glasses they don't automatically assume that I/we are educated and well read. People are still going to judge us by appearance and what we look like. So, I'm kind of distraught because I feel like for one, particularly my son, he is around a lot of female energy and female mindsets in a female environment. I feel like he is over-mothered and under-fathered. This changes his identity. It changed my identity being around my mom all the time, but I got what I call "saved" a little bit by the time I did get around my father and other men. I feel like I would have been super soft if I had been raised by my mother all my life.

At one point in time my dad came through and he was militant with me. That kind of toughened me up but if I hadn't gone to jail, I would have definitely been super soft. As I mentioned previously, I did have a time when I moved with my father in the 10th grade and that was a good pointe in my age coming out of middle school. I was just really hanging out with my friends, and I wasn't getting any girls. I really didn't know how to interact with females, and I still feel like I don't. My folks and I never sat down and talked to me about girls, not even my mom.

My upbringing was completely different from my American friends' households compared to my household. Like how my friends talked to their parents and how I talked to my parents and what I had to do for the day. Or even what my friends had to do for the day or what my mother would allow. I could always see the difference. So yeah, I'll say that my mom raised me more in love and my dad raised me more in discipline. So, I guess that had me evened out because of who I am and what I went through. The time I had with my father was important. My viewpoint is he is an ***hole, and he doesn't know how to talk to people. He has a hot temper and I got that from him. I feel like it's because I got beat and I didn't tell anybody, I held it in and suppressed it.

WORDS OF WISDOM

The most important thing is that you have to know who you are for one. I wish I had taken the time out to "gain self-knowledge." Secondly, I would tell him to really have protected sex. I feel as if there should be a questionnaire one should have when dealing with people or when you are about to go into a relationship. I think now one should have a list of expectations of what you expect from this person. Another list of what you are bringing to the table. What are you expecting from someone else? It's also important to know the person of interest background.

Like for a man we should ask a woman was her father in her life, how was their relationship, what was your upbringing like, what about your grandparents and do more getting to know one another. Not that you are judging, because I don't judge anybody, but I do observe and then use my observations to conclude then you can go from there. At that point you can see if that person can be compatible with you. No one is perfect but I can't expect to get with somebody and not expect them to have any prior dilemmas. There are a lot of unrealistic expectations.

More importantly I suggest having patience with your kids. One thing that used to really annoy me with my son's mom speaking on my personal experience is my annoyance of her frustration with the kids. I don't think I ever lost patience or got mad that they weren't eating something or if I have to tell them something one hundred times. I understand a lot of parents don't like to repeat things to their children but if they don't get it then they don't freaking get it! They are young! You can't have adult expectations and adult mentality expectations on a child. A child can be ten years old, and you expect them to think and operate like an adult? When my son was small, I used to get on my knees and talk to him.

There are a lot of things in parenting that would benefit from sitting down and reading and then applying the knowledge. This will allow you to get on a better plane with your children. People aren't doing it anymore. Everyone wants to be entertained by their children. No one wants to do the work because it is "work." No one wants to cut off the distractions. If I'm going to be a good parent, then that's what I'm going to be focusing on. If I'm a parent, then I need to be taking a parenting class. I'm a barber so I had to take a barbering class. If I'm a bus driver, then I must learn how to drive a bus. People aren't educating themselves in the field that they are in for the rest of their lives. If I'm a parent, then I'm a parent for the rest of my life. I knew I was going to be a parent for the rest of my life when I had my son fifteen years ago. This is a forever commitment. This isn't just taking care of you for a year, eight years, eighteen years. Nah!! I'm at my age of forty years old and my mother doesn't take care of me, but if I need something and I don't have it, she got me. I don't ask my mother for nothing but it's a known fact that she's there as a parent should I need her.

In a nutshell just knowing what you want in your partner when you are thinking about parenting makes a significant difference in how you are going to be able to raise your children.

"Mo"

I did not grow up with both of my parents in the household. I was raised solely by my father. I have two siblings, a brother and a sister and we have the same set of parents. My brother and I were raised together in the house by our father. My sister, however, was not in the household because she was raised by my aunt. She did not live in the house with us, but she spent time and visited with us on a regular basis.

Early on in my life, I really didn't have an idea about where my mom was, but I did know that she lived in the City somewhere. I got a chance to see her off and on, but it was a lot of bitterness between my parents. When I did get a chance to see her, I would say I was like ten or eleven years old, or something like that. However, I do know that earlier in my life it was not much contact. I would hear a lot of who she was, and you know how people tell you their interpretation of a person. So, I guess for me, my perception of my mother was what my father had told me. You know how it is, when people tell you something, you just believe it. It was until I was in my late teens or early adulthood, I didn't have a whole lot of understanding. Once you heard one story from my father and then on the other hand when I finally got the story from my mother it was different.

From my perspective, I had a pretty happy childhood. I think once I got to understand some of my makeup, because there were a lot of things, I was missing that my mother would have given me, especially being nurtured and compassionate. All the things that come from a mother. My daddy was kind of rough with his way of doing things. He was doing things the best way he could with the situation he was given.

101

Of course, growing up there were a lot of different feelings that I had to contend with. Such as Mother's Day; it wasn't one of those days I was happy with. Growing up I gravitated to a lot of my friends' mothers. I was the guy with the father whereas a lot of my friends' situations were just the opposite, they had their mothers and no fathers. So, their mothers became my mother.

My father did have a support system while raising us. I had an aunt that lived in the community. There were times when he had to work, and we would stay over at her house because we have a big family. As far as when we were growing up in the projects, everybody just looked out for everybody. I just know that my father did what he had to do to make sure that we had everything that we needed. You know, we had neighbors, aunts, and every now and then we would go to my grandmother's house. So yes, he did have a good support system, as far as I understood things.

MEMORIES

I think one of my most negative moments as a child was when my father was doing what he was doing as an adult. He lived his life, he did his drinking or whatever he did, but the most negative part was having to hear him talk about my mother during those times. It was always, "this was this" or "this was that" and "she ain't never do good." So, that's what I understood it to be.

The most positive memory was just growing up in a community where a lot of my friends were similar but still being able to be happy playing in youth sports because that was what we did. Even today I am still in contact with a lot of my childhood friends. Some of them go all the way back, like the dude that gave me my first bicycle, we are really good friends to this day.

Being a part of or even watching some incidents as I was growing up, had an impact on me. I think some of the acting out and being jive angry or going from zero to a thousand in a heartbeat, that kind of impacted me. Then, following behind an older sibling who laid a trail to everywhere you went, and you had to go behind him. Where he went to elementary school, I used to hear "oh you just like your brother…." And I was always out to prove them wrong. I was me. You know.

My brother was two years older than me and then I was one year older than my sister. I had some siblings that I found out about years later, My mother had two additional children with another man, but they were a lot younger than me. As for my brother and I we always had the normal sibling rivalry. We played hard and we fought a lot. He was himself and I was me. He was just wild. Our relationship was that of love, but we also had some moments when we couldn't stand each other. He would always remind me that he was my big brother. My sister and I have always been tight. Even to this day. We may not see each other for a while but when we get on the phone, we talk like it was just yesterday. A call between us can last like forty-five minutes to an hour easily. Our relationship on both ends I think has always been pretty good.

As far as my temperament growing up being the middle child. I wouldn't say I was as laid back as a middle child. I was into sports, you know jive shy for a minute, a little husky joker. I was just a middle child, whatever comes with that. Also being a middle child, I was caught up in paving my own way. It was like, you have to follow him, whereas my sister was on the other end of town. She was up there where my grandparents and my aunt were, and we were in the projects. It was two totally different atmospheres. Then I also grew up around my cousins who were into just about everything. After a certain age, I started getting into everything as well. I just knew early on that I wanted everybody to know I was me.

As far as my education, I don't think I excelled in school as much as I should have, but I passed every grade and graduated from high school. My brother, however, made it to the twelfth grade and decided that he was going to go into the military and of course my sister graduated. As for me personally, I just know that I could have done a lot better than I did. I believe I did just enough to get by. I passed in the subjects that I liked and some of the subjects I barely got by. I enjoyed school because I'm a people person at heart. I was also one of those dudes that had a lot of friends. You know when you play sports and coming up you had your rivalries all through the City. I had a lot of guys that I ended up going to high school with and that are still my friends today. I did go to college for a little while. It was trade school for a year then college for a year. The one thing I know now is that I wasn't prepared for the classes I took, which made a big difference in the outcome. I believe if I had been prepared academically, I probably would have done better, but that could have been a hit or miss. I just wanted the opportunity, and it was free.

BECOMING A FATHER

When I started dating a young lady, she already had a child. She was about six months old. I had to be in my early twenties. It is one of the best things that ever happened to me. Unfortunately, I don't think I was equipped at that time for what came with it. It was a little different dealing with someone who already had a child or having your own. It came with a lot of responsibilities making sure you get the things they needed. At that time, I was doing alright for myself, had a pretty decent job and went to work, but that took a curve.

My most difficult time was just being a father. You know people have expectations on you so sometimes it's hard to live up to. I think for me, I had to make sure not only was I being the best I could be, but I was still doing "my thing." I was still trying to run the streets and still trying to be responsible making sure I had all the things I could give. I don't know if I was doing it the right way. If there is such a thing as the right way. I think I could have been a lot better father than I was, if I didn't do some of the things that I was doing. So, some of the decisions that I made weren't healthy not only in my relationship but with my daughters as well.

At one point I was in my self-destruction mode. I was just running the streets thinking I was doing something slick. I was still in what was supposed to be a committed relationship with my daughter's mother. It was during this time that I had a son.

Honestly, to this day I don't think I ever said that I was having another baby. It just became evident, and it wasn't received well at all. It was known that I was doing what I was doing. No, I don't think it was received and I think it's still not even today. I'm not saying I think that person might be bitter, but she would never say it. I think the way I did what I did wasn't acceptable to my wife.

I know that there were plans and hopes derailed around that particular situation. I might have even sold the pipe dream to my child's mother because that's what I was doing at that time and where my head was. I was doing some real crazy mess back then. So, I don't know if it was my illusion or an illusion that I was selling. A situation came about after I did all of that and things became a back and forth, and running through the court system. The only thing that came out of it was that we had a son. That's about it but we are at least cordial now because we have grandkids now. I just believe that my state of mind, and how I was living, and what I was doing it was reckless for real.

Eventually I received help from the City police department. I had caught a charge and I had to sit down for a minute. My reality comparing my left hand to my right hand enabled me to choose to be with my right hand. I made some decisions that was better. One situation outweighed the other. Sitting down thinking about going through the changes of an active addiction and getting clean and just looking at my life. My life and what I was doing was crazy. So, I had to pray on some things, and I just chose wisely. After all of that, I did get married to the mother of my daughter. We have been married for 30+ years now.

Looking at co-parenting, with my wife's (biological) daughter, whom I wholeheartedly consider and love as my daughter, being in the same house from the beginning of our relationship, it wasn't as difficult to co-parent as it was with my son being in a different household. The situation stemming from where my son was tended to create a lot of chaos. When I say that, I am referencing the times of trying to visit, and having a mediator present to pick him up. Also, the calling back and forth created another level of situations with my wife. It was a lot to deal with. On the one hand, with my daughter, it was the best thing. It's just so funny, because at times I feel as if she is more like me than my own biological daughter.

In thinking about my son. I don't know if he harbors resentment or not. I do know there are some things he has said and that we have talked about over the years. However, that was a totally different and difficult task to deal with. Then have to deal with a person who really wasn't truthful and didn't want you to be a part of that situation at all. Even in the small things such as keeping me out of the loop with his educational needs, conferences, and not being inclusive as an emergency contact. Every time I turned around it was always another fight about something. It wasn't until he reached an age to be able to understand himself and see the picture for what it was.

I never had to worry or second guess if and when my son's mother had moved on with her life or if there were another man in her life that would be around to parent/co-parent with my son. From the beginning my son was just what he was…..my son. I did everything I possibly could through the years to make sure that he knew who I was and to remain a big part of his life. The only animosity that had anything to do with myself was surrounding the fact that my son was kept away from me and the untruths that were being told about me. It would affect us in such a way that once he would return to visit me, the work and the bonds that had begun to strengthen would have taken a slight hit with him returning as a different child with a different attitude toward me.

As for my bonus daughter, I never had any issues in any type of co-parenting with her paternal father. Unfortunately for him, but definitely fortunate for me, he never wanted to be a part of her life from jump street. His loss was my total gain.

GENERATIONAL TRAITS

What I feel as though I have taken from my upbringing into being a father is watching my father being a parent. I witnessed him changing his lifestyle. I realized I still had a lot of growing up to do. I was still angry about a lot of things.

I just didn't know what it was at the time. I think with him just being there was the most important thing. I don't know if I were always there as a parent in my mind but just physically being there from elementary school to junior high school, to high school, to college and graduations, I pulled my weight the best I could.

REGRETS

I just wish that I weren't so angry at times. It caused me to be abusive in some situations. Not only physically but verbally as well. I wish I could have been more tactful or had more patience. That is my biggest regret. I also wish that I had not allowed certain situations to overpower things. Sometimes when you are just not able to meet certain expectations that others put on you if you are being realistic. I do know that I didn't help in some of the situations.

TODAY IN SOCIETY

I don't think my girls have had too much to contend with regarding society. I feel as if with them having a strong mother in their background, I don't think it did as much as it did the damage with my son. He was just a different creature. He just feels entitled, whereas they learned early and captured the trait of earning what they wanted. They went to school and are both successful. He is just starting to come around and he reminds me of myself a lot in the aspect of being a late bloomer. It is starting to finally come to him what he needs to be doing because now he has kids of his own.

MY FEARS

I think in their teenage years, I feared that they would run into people or guys that was like me. I guess I really did want to protect them. I had to believe that whatever we instilled in them was the right thing and that they would do the right thing. They have always had a strong influence in their lives with their mother. My thing was I just wanted to always be there the best I could to make sure they had that level of protection that I knew would be needed. That's one of those things that you constantly work on because as they get older, they develop their own way of thinking and doing things. Sometimes you would hear or see it. Sometimes you can give suggestions and sometimes you have to just figure it out. I work harder with my son than I do with them because again, it was all laid out for them. The path was created for them. This is what y'all need to do, and this is how you do it. They were also told there wasn't going to be no whole lot of foolishness with boys. They were educated not just in school but at home about life as well. It was much easier for them, and I didn't have to do a lot; just be there to support. It was their mother.

My son was my biggest battle. He had periods when he wouldn't even pick up the phone. Then when he would pick up the phone it was when he wanted something. Then there is the realization of knowing when to cut things off and just say, "ok it's time for you to figure it out; I can't keep on helping you." Now it's, "dad I hear myself in you." Now all of the hundreds of times I have said things to him and now with two girls and a son, he is finding out that he is saying the same things to them.

You know the apple doesn't fall too far from the tree when you are looking at yourself. Especially with his own. I could never turn my back on him even when I was super pissed off with him. I just waited it out and prayed on it. I would let it take its' course and sooner or later he would come around and come with an apology. Things are definitely getting better than it had been between us. For example. You know what I like and what I don't want around me, but you test me. After I get on you about it, then you say, "you right." My foremost thought at that point is "you should have known I was right the first time." I have always told him "I ain't never told you nothing wrong." These are your decisions to make and want to do things right. I can't do it for you. I'm not doing no time for you or none of that. I think it's coming together for him though, just like it took me a minute.

DO OVER

I don't think I would want any do-overs in parenting because I probably wouldn't be who I am today. I know there are some things that I wish I could have done differently. I think I could have been a better husband at times because I know I did some things that were unacceptable. Not only to God but in a marriage. So, no do-overs, but I do wish I had done things differently.

WORDS OF WISDOM

To a younger me, I would say to trust God. I had a lot of doubts about what was going on in my life. My main question was, if it was such a powerful God then why all of these things were happening to me. I understand now how important it is to have him in your life. So, I would just say to trust and believe. My grandmother used to tell me this all the time, "it's gon' be alright." I believe that.

I also would use all of my resources. I would take advantage of things pertaining to education and some opportunities that I missed by being arrogant, bullheaded, being a militant and just not listening. I would be more consistent with the way I did things. I don't have many regrets today. I really don't. I just know I am who I am because of who He is. I have come a long way.

All that I have said I would also tell that to another young man coming to me for advice. In addition, I would make sure to let him know that nobody owes you anything. Everything you get is because you earned it. Our generation had people that were for us even in our mess when we were doing wrong, and they always talked to us about doing right. For the most part we got it right, but it took some time. The generation that is up to bat now lacks respect and they think they are entitled, and they think everybody owes them something. No one owes you anything.

When I was at a low point in my life, I went through a job situation, and I was down on myself. I honestly felt like I didn't get the support that I deserved as a man. I found God! It's just that simple. I don't understand a lot about it, because I am still on a young journey, but I kept on saying to God, "why do you keep on giving these people stuff and you are not giving it to me?" Then after talking a lot with my dad and my pastor, I had to understand that it was going to come but it was going to come when He wanted me to have it. If it had come when I thought I needed it, I would have messed it up. I strive to maintain my peace of mind. I am hoping one day to be able to retire but if it's in my genes (and I am like my dad who is still working) I will be working for a good while.

I would also tell young people to invest in themselves. When I say that, I mean, save money. Invest in savings plans, 401 plans and retirement. At the time that I was told to do it, if I had done so, I would be sitting pretty right now. At a young age, I thought I had more time and I'm not making that type of money to do that right now. I just didn't look at it that way.

Overall, make sure you recognize who your real friends are. Listen to the words of wisdom and nuggets that are given to you and if you can't use it right now, just tuck it away because you will eventually.

"THE UNKNOWN"

GROWING UP

My life started off with growing up with both of my parents in the same household. My parents were in a long-term relationship, not married. They eventually separated so it was just my mom, my siblings and me. By the time I was in the sixth grade, my mother reconnected with her husband now, which I call Pops. For me, it was like a half and half growing up. My biological father was in and out of my life during my childhood years and even through high school. That was a childhood sore growing up for me.

I have two siblings, a brother, and a sister, which grew up in the same house as me and I am the youngest of the three of us by my mother. My oldest sibling, my sister, also has a different biological father. My pops is the biological father of my brother, my mom's middle child. He and my mom married one another when I was in high school in the eleventh grade. They have been married about twenty-three years now.

I had a happy childhood as it relates to my mom because she provided stability for us no matter what. I admired her strength as she was a single mom for a good while, making it happen. My oldest siblings always say that she let me get away with murder as I got older when it came to curfews and stuff like that. However, she worked hard and made sure that she provided for us. We grew up in the projects and on any given day you couldn't tell us that we were not poor because I had the same things as my classmates that stayed out in the bougee areas. She always taught us how to be independent. However, when it came to my father being in and out of my life, that's when the roller coaster of sadness and everything would come into play because he was in and out. One thing

I can say is that my mom never kept any of us away from our fathers. It didn't matter how long he was gone, whenever he returned it was as if we had been together forever. I guess during that time I really needed him.

I used to envy my peers who used to have their fathers there at school for parent nights, the father/son breakfast, and other things. I didn't get to experience any of that with my biological father in my schooling. So, it impacted me greatly. I used to find myself longing and wishing that he were there.

On the flip side of that, once my pops came into my life, things changed for me. I took on the mindset of not really caring if my biological dad came or not. My pops taught me a lot of things from the time he showed up all the way to my adulthood. He is a quiet and humble man. I watched him and observed how he treated my mom.

At the same time, from watching my biological dad there were things that he did that I always said that I would never do and didn't wanna do. He was an alcoholic and on drugs. I remember going to family functions as a kid and we would have to leave because things would get that bad with him. It would get to the point where the family didn't want us there.

So naturally, when my pops stepped into play, that was a breath of fresh air for me. I have always been one to observe everything including his mannerisms. It was something that I modeled. From my mom's end everything was excellent. She was always upbeat and showed up for us. For me, I never missed a field trip, or an overnight trip when it came to school or to church. I was always present on the college tours and everything else that came up. Some of those trips as a single mom were expensive and she made sure that I had money to take with me to spend. All the trips that you go on in school from Camp Thunderbird for a week, Nassau Space

Center in Alabama for four days, the Outer Banks, and Disney World. Anything that I wanted to participate in while in school she made sure that it happened.

I graduated high school and went on to college. I have a bachelor's degree in general education K-8 with a dual in Special Education K-12. I am an educator as an Exceptional Children (EC) Resource teacher in a middle school. My students who fall under the EC category and struggle academically, come to me for resources to provide them with the extra assistance and the push they require to be successful scholars in school. They do change classes with their peers but one of their blocks is dedicated to me in my classroom. In addition to that I also support the classroom teacher in helping the student with whatever content area they are struggling in. We work together to keep them on target, so they are not left behind. Hence, 'No Child Left Behind.' I am also currently in grad school and it's kicking my *$$!! I am doing all online classes now and expect to be completed in the Spring 2024.

MEMORIES

My most memorable negative moment was being molested as a child. Even in relationships now I have a wall up. I try to block it out, but it is still there. That memory is there. Then later in my adulthood I learned that the same individual that was molesting me was also molesting my niece. I just learned in the last year that it was happening to the both of us at that time. It was something that I kept in for a long time and didn't feel comfortable talking about. I looked at myself as if there was something wrong with me because this was when I was in the third and fourth grades. It still impacts my life at times. I never sought out any type of counseling or therapy. I block it out a lot. It's hard to explain but I get through it.

My most positive memory from my childhood that has impacted my life was during the time my parents were together. My mom's biological mother stayed in a large northeastern state. I remember hearing we were going to go and all I could think of was how far away it was. I do remember distinctly us being on a ferry ride. We went there for a vacation for a week. Again, I remind you that we were poor, but you wouldn't know it. I was fortunate enough to leave from the projects, my community, the city, and state I grew up in during those times as a child. Yet my peers were not able to do so. I just remember all the museums we took the time to see. We were just in awe of everything.

BECOMING A FATHER

It was the year 2000; I was eighteen going on nineteen and had graduated high school when I found out I was going to be a father. I was not in a relationship with anyone, but I did have relations with a young lady I had been working with. We were both preparing to leave for our respective colleges in the Fall. I received a text message from the young lady stating she had something to tell me. She went on to say that she was pregnant. My response to her was that we have to figure it out because we are both literally getting ready to leave to go away to school.

We both went on to college and lost contact with one another. Needless to say, I was not around for the birth of that child. Actually, it was years later, about twenty-two years, that we reconnected. It was a weird situation because we were not kids any longer. We were adults at this point. I have had past relationships, have other kids and this is her only child. I was able to meet my son finally and we are building a relationship with one another. They do live in another state, but I did go out to the West coast last year where they live. It was good to see him face to face but right now everything is communicated via phone calls.

I did have the initial conversation with him and owned up to my part in not being in his life. I explained how his mom and I were young; went away to separate colleges and we lost contact with each other. His mom was very open and honest and confirmed to him that this indeed is what happened. I told him that we cannot go back and patch up, redo, or fix the past but that we can start over from here fresh and new. We are willing to put in the work and embrace the situation and build from here. The blessing in this is my son is being receptive to me.

I do feel bad about the lost time because I know how I felt growing up and not having my biological father as a constant in my life as a child. I can only imagine what my son has felt or is feeling now. My father was in and out of my life, and I missed all my son's. I even had to mention to both about the time when I went to her parents' house, and they were not even living there any longer. The ability for her to be able to reach out after she was able to search and find me on social media has allowed me to be able to have a part in my son's life. He is my twin as well as my dad's twin.

In 2005, I was in a long-term relationship with my girlfriend at the time and that's when she told me that we were expecting a baby in December. As history does tend to repeat itself, I found out through a text message again. We made a conscious decision at that point to get married to make things right. That year was a very joyful year. Everyone from family, friends and colleagues were very excited and rooting for us. Fast forward to November, my then wife ended up in the hospital due to her placenta rupturing. This resulted in her being admitted for a couple of weeks. The morning our son was born, I was at home, preparing for a field trip for the students at my school and I get a phone call letting me know to get to the hospital because the baby was on the way.

When our son was born, he ended up in the Neonatal Intensive Care Unit (NICU). As time progressed, he grew and showed us so much and so many things that you wouldn't expect a newborn to do. It was a joy filled time. However, he was not able to survive more than eleven days old before he passed away. It was really devastating to lose a son that young. I couldn't figure out which part was more difficult from dealing with the loss, comforting my wife, or making the arrangements for a funeral for such a young and innocent life. Being a young parent and having to carry that burden was more than overwhelming. That left a big void in our hearts and our faith was definitely tested. We have always heard that we are not supposed to question God but we're human and the human side of us wanted to know why this was allowed to happen to us. At the young age that we were, we were excited about becoming parents and preparing for the birth of our child and to have it taken away in the blink of an eye is sorrowful.

The holidays are hard since his passing was during the month of December. So, during that time and years after, we try and do something to honor his memory. We do so by giving to others. I continue to do that to this day. Again, I want to reiterate that we were young and had not even developed the life skills to deal with most adult-like situations. So, with this traumatic event, we grew angry and bitter at times individually and collectively, but we continued to push through it all.

In September of 2006, we found out that we were expecting another baby. The pregnancy makes it past the first trimester and into the second trimester when we find ourselves at the hospital being admitted again for premature labor. She had a hard time holding and carrying her babies. The physicians explained all that medical terminology and the test results and informed us that this baby, another son, was not going to make it either and that his lungs were too underdeveloped. Faced with preparing to bury him was like snatching a bandage off a freshly stitched up wound. This put a strain on our relationship, and our marriage for several different reasons and we ended up separating after that.

In 2009, after being separated from one another for a while, a mutual friend of ours had passed away. I reached out to my wife to make sure she was in the loop of this information I had received. We then just started talking to one another and spending time together on a more frequent basis. By January 2010, I was at a Dr. Martin Luther King concert at a church, and I get a text that says, "what do you see?" It was an ultrasound. I was blown away and said, "TWO?" There was A and a B. She said, "yeah we're having twins." At this time, I'm thinking to myself, "awwww hell." We weren't even trying but thinking back to a conversation that my mom had told me about. One of the Mother's from the church had prophesized to my mom that "God showed her that the next pregnancy is gonna be twins." This was told to my mom in the latter part of 2006 to early 2007. So, it was not surprising to me to receive this confirmation from my wife.

Even though we were still legally separated, living in different cities, I still made sure I was there for every appointment that she had. We told the doctors that we needed them to do everything they could to keep this as a viable pregnancy to make sure these babies made it because "I'll be damned if it was gonna be a third and a fourth loss." They did assure us that at that time, in 2010, technology had come a long way since 2005 and 2006, respectively. The doctors were able to perform a Cervical Cerclage (known as a cervical stitch) to keep her cervix closed. Once this procedure was done, she was able to carry the twins up to a safer gestational date. Even though they were premature, which we were informed that most multiples are, they were born with no major issues. The conversation I had with the doctors after the birth of the twins was revisited and I reminded them of our path and that we were not going to leave the hospital without the twins. We were able to leave the hospital once the twins were able to meet all the medical criteria for premature births. They are the joy of my life.

Moving along, my wife and I are still separated. However, unexpectedly, in 2014, we have another daughter. This pregnancy was a smooth one with no hiccups at all.

Unfortunately, as far as being able to co-parent with my ex-wife, I am unable to see our children. We went from the children coming with me every single weekend for visitation to abruptly none. In 2018, all of it just came to a complete stop. No matter how much I try to see them, I am unable to do so. I am frustrated with the entire situation because I do pay child support regularly through a court order, yet I am unable to see them. I have even tried to fight it in the court system but there were several false scenarios painted against me.

The stories or accusations that were presented against me ranged from funny to outrageous. One of the most talked about untruths was how the children were hungry when in my presence. Now, everyone who really knows me, knows that this belly I have is always hungry and being fed. On top of that, I was living in my parents' home at the time and my mom would always cook meals for the kids. My mother has been a tremendous support to me this entire time. In addition, it was said that they were scared of me, and I was abusive to them. I can adamantly say that I never put my hands on my kids.

It's just mind blowing to me how some women can use the children against the father in a court of law. Let me say this. It has never been a situation that I have never been in my kids' life, I have always wanted to be there and provide for them, and I can't. I will say this. The whole child support thing angers me because I don't get to see them. There's no valid reason for me not to be able to. When I try and fight for my right to see them, there is a rebuttal with a bunch of lies that makes it so much easier for the courts to go against my favor. After fighting and not getting any lead way, I asked my attorney whether this would be hard to fight and he said, yes it would be due to the number of allegations and supposed evidence she had. I finally got to the point where I just told me lawyer that I would leave it alone. I just will never understand why I am not able to see them, pay child support faithfully and their mom can still request increases in the monthly allotments that she already receives.

I will say this. In 2020, she did reach out to me and asked did I want to see the kids. Of course, my response was, "uhm yeah, it was never me." So, from about September to December of that year, she allowed me to see them. On Christmas Eve, in 2020, I had purchased cell phones for all three kids. My family had purchased gifts for them and by mid-January I had stopped hearing from them on their phones. I would text their mom and ask her to tell the kids to reach out to me or answer my calls or text messages. Then I would reach out to them and wouldn't get a response back. This went on for a while with no change. I have not heard from them, and I have not seen them since. It has all not just angered me, but it has had me dealing with all types of emotions, including depression. My hope and prayer at this point is that as the children get a little older and they can make decisions on their own, that they will not have so much negative information downloaded into them, and that they will want to reconnect with me again. It is very stressful. I have missed a lot of special events and milestones just in these years.

The fact that when a person has their own feelings, emotions and issues yet use them to place their children in a position they don't fully understand, is too confusing for me to wrap my head around.

GENERATIONAL TRAITS

Unfortunately, the things that I have felt I always learned as I was growing up and carried with me and planned to use when raising my own children have had to be put on the back burner. The good thing about all that I have and continue to learn is that I am at least able to put it back into the lives of my students. Through my work at my place of employment as well as out in the communities, I have a big impact on children that do not belong to me, but I am unable to have that same type of impact on my own. The only saving grace that I have right now is being able to see the gratitude of other kids of what I have poured into them.

REGRETS

I feel as if the path that things have gone within my parenting has had the opportunity to place a lot of regrets in my whole thought process. I do know that I have no regrets whatsoever when it comes to having my kids. The regret I would say is just the relationship along with all the twists and turns with their mother. I regret that things could not have been handled differently. Especially since the two of us started out as high school sweethearts and kept finding our way back to one another. Even with every separation within our marriage we would go down different paths only to find one another again. The biggest challenge has been not only just to see them but to love them as they so deserve.

DO OVER

The only thing that I would change regarding being a father is to be there to witness each one of my children's milestones. By not being there and missing so many things has left a void. Missing the first days of school and different promotions in their education has hurt me and I am sure it has hurt them as well.

WORDS OF WISDOM

Dear Brother. My charge to you is to make each day great as they come. Love on those around you. If you are becoming a father, then prepare yourself for the unexpected and the unknown. Those days will come, and challenges will come. However, remember to stand up to be that man that God would have you to be in your kids' life, in your family's life and in the community as a young brother. My charge to you is to live each day as if it's your last because we don't get back certain opportunities. Just make sure that you are there for your kids and don't allow those dark days to outweigh the sunlight. Never let the negativity or the brick wall that you may run into deter you from the ultimate goal. Whatever that may be in your life. Will challenges come? Yes. Will punches be thrown? Yes. However, you can still come out on top and on the winning side.

"MILEK"

Both my mother and father were present in the household while I was growing up. My parents have been married for over fifty years. I am the youngest of three children, and there is a nine- and ten-year difference in ages between my sisters and myself. I come from a very large family with a lot of aunts, uncles, and cousins along with extended family. I never had to look far for any type of nurturing needed, whether it be from male or female role models or images. That in itself made a big difference in my life.

My mother and father were very well known in the community where we lived and where they raised us. So, in addition to having a great childhood, there was also some great expectations that came with that. There was a certain way that you really had to carry yourself.

MEMORIES

There were moments in my childhood that I won't say were negative but there were things that happened in life that affected me. When it comes to my grandfathers, I don't recall my mother's father ever being around or involved with me or my sisters, so I never had a relationship with him. I found out later that he was a professional Black soccer player in the area. This fact is interesting to me because a lot of people know me from playing basketball, but I was originally a soccer player from childhood through high school. To know that you had a grandfather who was also that person within the sport, yet he never saw you play. It didn't really affect me because I didn't know him.

However, I remember my father's father as this image. He was this cool, dark-skinned, cigar toting man. Everybody in the City that I grew up in knew him. He and I had a really cool relationship. He was a leader of a very prominent social chapter within the City. That also was something that I was known for, being the grandson of him. Because of whom he was and how I looked at him, it would have been really cool to have had him in my life in the later years but he passed away. It would have been really nice to have had him around during my high school years so that he could see the things I did. Good and bad. Other than those aforementioned things, I can't really say that I had any negative experiences growing up.

The most prominent positive thing from my childhood that has stayed with me to this day was anytime I was with my cousins. Both my mother and father sides are huge. For instance, one of my uncles that lived in an apartment, my cousins and I would stay the night over there. We would all be just piled up on each other. It was just fun. Everyone knew that you came to my house for wrestling events. Just being around my family; being around my cousins, that's the reason why I am who I am today, and I carry things a certain way now. It probably wasn't until I was a teenager when I was able to understand who a cousin was and who was a brother or a second cousin. We just weren't raised that way. Even now, when I have conversations with my significant other, and they start talking about second and third cousins, I cut that off because I don't believe in that. I don't know anything about that, and I can't tell you who is first or second to me. All I know is that it's family.

I have been surrounded by solid marriages and black love my entire life. My parents' friends were also people who were/are married for years. Some of the fellas that I have in my life as a big brother or little brother or whatever the case is, their households were the same way. Their mother and father have been married just as long as my parents have been. So, I didn't have to go far to see this is what marriage is. This is what it looks like and this is how you conduct yourself. This is what comes with it and the sacrifices. I didn't have to look far for that at all. I don't know if that was intentional on my parents' end, but it was what it was. It seemed like growing up, everybody's parents were married. I only remember one cousin's household that was different and, in his instance, as a child growing up, you didn't know the difference.

I have about eleven aunts and uncles. I only have one uncle that I don't really have a relationship with. A couple of my uncles have passed, and I have one uncle now who reminds me of my father as far as marriage and family. However, it wasn't always that way. As far as my childhood goes, the men of the church that also grew up with my father as well played a big part in my life. Whether it was me going over to their house because their son or daughter was in my age group or my sisters'. Their sons and daughters were so close that we were always together. We were all so close that this one particular uncle and aunt were not my bloodline, yet I never knew that they were not really related until I was a teenager. Because when something would happen or my parents wanted to go out, it was just said to us, "y'all going over your uncle and aunt's house." Or even when I was a kid and wanted to go sledding, their son, who I always thought was my cousin, would come and pick me up and take me to the school in order to go sledding.

So, these men were always involved in my life whether it was in a church setting or whatever the case may be. They corrected me just like they did their children. So did their wives. Even my mother's best friend who was a single woman carried things the same way. Any adults that I was around, they were an extension of my mother and father. It was understood that I needed to listen to them and act accordingly. Going a step further and going beyond couples, it was just positive Black images surround me.

I attended public school in the County of my residence for elementary and middle schools. Due to my popularity in sports along with some writing samples I had done and submitted it to a Black male counselor. Unbeknownst to me he had put my work in the hands of a scout for a private school and put me on their radar. My counselor called me into his office one day and tells me he wanted to 'speak with me about an opportunity that you have, and I want to talk to your parents about it'. After the conversation with my parents the door was opened for me to enter into high school at a private school.

If there was one event that changed my life and added substantially to it, it was going to a private school. Being in that private school I was surrounded by a population that was about 80% white, 5% Black and then the remainder 15% was made up of a melting pot of other races. I had to learn how to navigate through the cultural dynamics. From there I went to a HBCU. So, I went from a college preparatory institute to an HBCU where numbers within the various cultures were reversed ultimately. I did my four years there. Although I did not finish, I am proud to say that I did not because it had a lot to do with my journey professionally later on down the road.

I am twenty-three years into my profession. I don't think it was something that I set out to do initially, but it wasn't until years later that I came to realize that it was instilled in me. Being under my father and watching him always work with the youth in the church, taking folks places and things like that and it came naturally. When I started working with the population that I was working with at that time, it just came as natural as something I had been doing all along. It came to me with a level of patience and understanding for them and on top of that it was fun.

You realize that when it comes to working with children, it's just like with any other profession (and I make sure that I say the word profession) even when I am training others because it is a profession and not everyone can do it. It's just like with anything else, you learn your first layer of working with this product. In my case the product is a child. Then you start learning more by understanding this is how a child thinks, this is how they act or more importantly this is how you can help a child. Then comes the world of special needs. Once you get to that world and you start understanding and valuing it, and you get past the behaviors, you realize that you are dealing with young geniuses. You can't see it because the world has set us up not to see it socially. However, once you start working with them you realize that this child is a genius. So now, you are infatuated with their intelligence, and you want to keep working with them. Then once they realize that you see how smart they are then it's, "alright let me stop biting you," or "let me stop kicking you."

Being able to work with that population that just really kept me and then somehow, someway without me seeing it coming it just spilled into community work. Then it became making sure these children were given the attention and care once they left the four walls of our schools. The next thing is to think about what is happening to this kid over the weekend and what is happening in his community. So, from there and those questions, it led me to community work. Then it led to training and at that point it became a lot more to me of training people about what I saw in kids and do for the community what I have been able to do and find the resources and putting yourself in a position where you can have a seat at the table. In my position now I have a seat at the table, and I don't get told what policy is and is not. I tell people what policy can be.

I have put my work in over the years. The biggest criticism that I get is that I don't tell my story enough. I have had staff say to me, "I heard in a training that you did such and such." I have to admit to them at that point, "yes I did that." The repeated question is always the same of, "how come I never tell anybody." However, for me, it's just work. This is just what you do. It's almost like a testimony. You start telling people because you never know who you are going to touch but again, the people that I came under in my profession were not like that. They just did the work. Whatever needed to be done, got taken care of. Even my father with the work that he has done his whole life. He doesn't brag about it; it just gets done. So, I can proudly say that's where I get it from.

BECOMING A FATHER

I found out that I was going to be a father to a child of my own when I was twenty-three years old. So, biologically speaking, my daughter was born by the time I turned twenty-five. My first set of emotions definitely included fear. This is always something that any of us deal with anytime we are delving into the unknown or anything that you have never done before. I will say because of past decisions I made in my life; I felt this need to have this child as if it would right some of my wrongs from poor choices in the past. Funny how the mind works when rationalizing decisions.

During this time, I was also in a relationship for about a year or two with a young lady who already had a daughter that was not mine biologically. I chose to play a fatherly role in her life due to her own father not being as present or involved as he should. As we know, the absence of a father always affects the child in one way or another. It left a void to be filled and I stepped in to fill it.

There were issues that I faced in doing so but I had to learn to deal with certain situations. You can watch people every day and see how they handle things, but it is different when it comes to the time for you to do it. There are only so many times that you can watch a child with their bookbag packed, sitting on the edge of the bed waiting for a parent to come that you know is not going to show or is going to have some excuse for why they can't be there on time. At some point you have to make the decision to stop allowing the child to be disappointed because an adult can't understand the importance of putting your child first. Then there is the scenario of every time the child gets dropped off and they are not with the parent but with the grandparent(s). After a while of attempting to go out with my lady friend and you just feel in the back of your mind that something just doesn't feel right. That's the upbringing that comes into play for me. From the times that you experienced things or even saw things and then later down the road you realize something is amiss and it is all because that's not what you saw or experienced yourself growing up. We were still learning to be parents ourselves and were far from perfect but one thing we did know was that we needed to start including both children in our family outings to put a stop to some of the disappointment she was experiencing.

Once my youngest child came along there was definitely a change. The scenario was their mother, the oldest child who was six years older, my daughter and myself. We find ourselves in a dynamic that I actually try and talk to young folks about. When two people live together, whether you are married or not, you find yourselves taking on roles and responsibilities. I am expecting you to be that mother

133

dynamic and you are expecting me to be that father dynamic as far as heads of the household and we are learning through trial and error on top of that. When she had her first child she was in high school, and she was wherever she was mentally at that point and now here we are trying to figure out how to make all of this work. There were some really great times and there were some stressful times and some arguing going on. It was all just a growing process.

Let me say this carefully. Kids are kids. What you went through with yours as far as them being a newborn, really isn't too much difference between anyone else. It's the parents. We were learning how to be parents. She had things going on with her. I was still learning how to be a parent and professionally I was still trying to figure out what my moves were career-wise. We were twenty-four years old and trying to figure it out.

As I was saying previously, when my bio daughter came into the picture there was a shift in things. On any given day initially, we may have been getting the diaper bag ready, getting the baby dressed, we were getting ourselves dressed and about to make some moves and yet our oldest daughter's biological father still has not shown up nor have we heard from him to come and pick her up. Then there were the times that we may have dropped her off at her grandmother's house to wait for him to come pick her up and he never showed his face and ended up staying the entire weekend. The conversation between the two of us (her mom and I) became more about whether we could have just kept her with us instead of putting her through all of the waiting around and ultimately being let down.

At the time we were building relationships with my family and friends and just realized enough was enough. It was then that we came to the conclusion that the four of us needed to move as a family. We agreed that if the absent parent truly wanted a relationship with his daughter, then he needed to put forth a little bit more effort.

A lot happened in the five years or so that we were together. Our relationship was somewhat back and forth for the most part for about three years or so. By that time, we separated.

Eventually her mother married someone in the military. There were times when her husband was stationed overseas or on another coast. By the time my biological daughter was in the first grade, they moved to Korea. It was during those times that I feel as though our bonds became closer and our roles became more defined. When they had both daughters, it was all on them regarding responsibilities. I had to get myself to a point to trust mom and stepdad to take care of them.

However, during this transition of being a parent that is not able to be with my daughter daily, I opted to take some matters into my own hands. I sought out some legal processes in order to solidify myself in my daughter's life. I already knew what would come out of me seeking any type of joint custody. However, it was more important that I stay a part of her life with minimal complications as opposed to not be a part of her at all. Initially my daughters mother was not happy about my decision to take legal action and it definitely did not help our relationship. At that time in my mind, I felt it was because she believed she was in control, and I held all of the cards. Honestly, society also plays into that as well. They will have a man thinking that he has no cards to play. So, of course I had to be the one agreeing and saying "okay", "whatever you say". I had to put things into perspective and had also started seeking advice from men who were handling their business as fathers. They challenged me with questions such as, "is your business straight?" and "do you have somewhere to live?" and "financially can you provide support?" and "you have to make sure that your stuff is together first." Lastly, I was told, "if there are certain boxes that you can check off, then here is what you can do." I wasn't going in there trying to take my child away. I felt the odds were already stacked against me as a young black male in the judicial system and it was a female child involved.

I think I was fortunate enough and educated on how the system works. If you understand that you can work within it and you can get what you need. I remember I was living in an apartment, going online, looking up a custody agreement, and printing it out. For about a week while I was at work, I went over it and customized it, retyped it, and took it to our court session. I used that as my guide, clearly stating here are the things that I am asking for. I told them that I wasn't asking for anything out of the norm, but I am asking for equity. I am asking for the things I need to stay in my child's life, and I came prepared to articulate those points professionally.

I sat in that court room, and I watched. I saw guys come in there and tell them what they were and weren't going to do or tell them what they couldn't do. I even saw a guy in there with one of the largest, most expensive receipt books showing all of the extras that he had been purchasing. Immediately, the judge stopped him from speaking on it explaining that it was extra, and it would be considered gifts because nothing had been established. You have to be prepared and take some time to educate yourself. My goal was always to stay a part of my children's life and to support them the best way I could and to support their mother as well. Not just financially but to make sure that she gets the same opportunities that I get. The whole thing for me was that she can call the shots when they were with her, and I can do the same when they are with me.

In my opinion, the biggest complication that we had was us being young. In hindsight, I can see now that there were things that I did I'm sure she didn't like. Just as there were things, I didn't like that she did. Those things were a big part in us ending the way we did. Of course, we each have our own version of what happened. Either way, it happened. Because of the way it happened, the communication between us wasn't the best. I think on both sides we made decisions individually and did things that led the other person to feel the repercussions. I can say that with confidence because as co-parents now and understanding what that means, we don't have those issues. The difference now is that we communicate. Again, there were things that she was going through that drove her decisions. There were also things that I was going through as well. The biggest thing for me was forgetting why she did what she did or whatever the case was. What affected me the most was looking back on my childhood and how great it was. I was surrounded by nothing but successful Black men who were fathers. I'm not talking about professionally or how much money anyone had. I am talking about great fathers who worked hard in keeping their families together and I couldn't do that. I felt that I had failed. That's what affected me the most. That's what really fractured me as a man.

There were three different Milek's that you got as a result of that. In the summertime everyone knew that I was Milek, the father because my girls were home. From nine to five I was Mr. M. There's not a child, kid, or personality that I couldn't handle, and I dove all the way into my work. After hours I was a different beast. I can look back now and say because I felt like I felt as a father, I still needed to cope with that. So, I was out of control. I was off the hook. Not only was my world turned upside down, but it was such a big blow to my ego. It hit me physically, spiritually, and emotionally. If I wasn't doing the dad thing or if I wasn't doing the work thing, then I was out and about. I was drinking and going from woman to woman. What I grew to understand and what I don't think that people get, but as a parent who has the child primarily, I don't think it's understood from where the other parent is; you have to flip that switch off and on. I had to flip that switch for when I am a father for two months out of a year. Then to be able to deal with the absence of my child or children I had to cut that switch off because emotionally it's hard. You go from buying spaghetti-o's at the grocery store, saying prayers, going to your best friend and your cousins birthday parties and more. Then all of a sudden, you have to send your kids back.

So now all of that is done. Then I just return back to my new coping mechanisms. This made it easier for me to forget. It was almost like an out of sight out of mind thing. It's definitely different when your kids live in the same city. This is why I find it hard to understand when you are in the same city or vicinity as your kids, and you can't interact with them or have that relationship with them. My girls were in another country on the other side of the world. So, there was no "oh next weekend I'm going to get them." That's where it was really hard for me because once August hit and they get back on that plane, I'm flipping that switch. That's how I chose to cope with it all.

Once the girls returned to the area to be with me the roles were reversed and they in turn had to trust and allow me room to be dad to take care, provide and account for everything pertaining to them. It was a shift with them being with me for the summers and it became me and my girls. That's how it was known to everyone around me. When the summer comes, it's just me and the girls. There was a timeframe that I would not be involved with anyone because I wanted to focus on being with my daughters and building our relationships. Basketball has always played a big part in our relationship. During those summer months, we were together, and everyone was dribbling a ball for someone, going to gyms, practices, and games. That's really where I believe they both saw what dad was about and where we fit in. They saw how a dad is supposed to interact and the sacrifices that he should make for his family.

In the beginning, it was very difficult. It was difficult for a couple of reasons. My immediate circle of 'fellas' were all married and were all fathers. So now, I'm hanging and they're (my fellas and their wives) are together. I have become that friend who is a single dad. That in itself is weird and then you have everyone trying to hook you up. What made it more difficult was the fact that I did not have a relationship of any sort with my daughters' stepfather. We had no type of rapport. The only thing that we knew about one another was what was told to us by a third party, and it wasn't good. I couldn't say whether or not he was a good man or a bad man. How he was brought into my world wasn't a positive situation from the beginning. That's all that I had to go off of. It was very challenging. What helped was as the time went on the interaction with my daughters and the way they were coming back home talking about their experiences. He and I talked about this at a later time and because of this, I started to let my guard down a little bit but initially it was difficult.

It wasn't as if another man was raising my child because my daughters are still coming home to me. I never bought into the cliché about another man. It was simply that I did not know him. I just knew that when I would see him, I would associate him with the issue that I had with mom at that time. It was an issue that just would not resolve itself at first. As things go on you have to be the mature one and that was hard too because now, I have to show my girls that everything's good.

Honestly, sometimes I didn't want to be the mature one. When they came home from Korea, they were home for a longer period of time. So, we were able to get back to a more normal dynamic of every weekend and get a better grasp of the co-parenting thing. Our relationships were able to be built with stronger bonds and I didn't have to cut that switch off and on. I've never been denied my daughters. Ever. There has never been a situation where my children had been used against me. I never had to endure the statement of "no you can't come and see them." There's always been a recognition of me being a good father. That helps too.

With them being back in the area, my father role was able to be stretched out and be more consistent. That's when it got to a point where I could honestly say to myself that this is who I am, and I like this person. Once in that mindset, I was able to start to grow more into that role and I realized that being in Korea for those three years was necessary. For one, the kids got a great experience but for two, I needed it. I told their mother once that I needed her gone and I needed him gone. I needed to go through all of the stuff that I did because when they came back, we were better.

A lot of that stuff we were able to put behind us and learn to co-parent better (because we had not mastered it yet). Co-parenting is a great deal harder than regular parenting. My daughters' mother and I eventually got to a place where we were comfortable enough to hang out together and watch games as friends. Her husband and I were also able to get to the point where we were able to build our relationship with one another. It was almost like you see on the TV. Here comes dad to pick up the kids from stepdad kind of scenarios. We were able to start putting those types of things in place. That was good. Me and their mom still had some things that we had to work out but for me I was in a better space where I was able to let those things happen and I think she was too.

My oldest daughter, who I still treat as mine, is living with me to this day. She is employed and works close to my home. So, it works for both of us. There is no type of negativity between her mother and me.

Where we are now, we still have our moments but for us I think that we have learned how to co-parent. When I talked about that switch of turning it on and off in the past, it doesn't exist in the same sense as it did before. When the girls are with their mom , I trust that they will make the right decisions and that they will do what needs to be done and we communicate in order to fill me in. When they are with me for the summer months, it's the same thing. When they moved back from a southwestern state where they had been living to my hometown, everybody moved back. So, everyone is here. There is no separate decisions because we are all in the same area and we have to make decisions together. We have to communicate and co-parent in the same vicinity. This means that our rapport had to be good and that was something we had to work on. With them coming back to the area that I was already in, and already had life set up and things in motion, everything had to be reevaluated.

I remember the oldest one coming home and the plan was for her to come home and go to school. Well, I ended up getting her a job where I work at and my thought process was, ok you have a job but now you have to get to work, and I can't take you. So, I wanted to get her a car and I didn't talk that over with her mother and when she found out that I bought her a car it was like WWIII. Yet for me, I'm thinking along the terms of this is what she needs. Her issue was that I didn't talk to her about it. That's where our co-parenting and everything really came into play with having to communicate and talk through things. Especially when my youngest daughter was in high school because she was a great deal more dramatic than her older sister. My youngest was the one that we had to go through all of the TV drama stuff that teenage girls go through, and we had to be on point with that. Oh, we had our moments because whenever she and I didn't communicate about something we had our arguments.

So that was the next chapter for us. At this point I think we are doing well, but it wasn't easy. However, you don't realize it when you are going through. Like for instance our oldest daughter may tell us she wants to do something now and I look at her and ask, "did you talk to your mother?" Then it is the same thing for her mother when she is asked to do something, she will in turn say, "did you talk to your father?"

Another avenue that has helped us to start putting things into perspective was because her husband has a dynamic with his child's mother currently. They are where we were. It's interesting because we try and stay on the same page because now, we watch them go through what we've been through. Then it's like, oh my gosh, were we that bad? It's just different dynamics. I help with their daughter. When all three of our daughters would fly into the area together, I received each of them off the plane and made sure that everybody arrived to where they needed to go. Her husband was very appreciative of this gesture. I have had to respond to him, "no problem because I know that my daughter has been in Korea with you." So now we have gotten to the point where we trust one another with each other's kids. As far as fathers, he and I have a fatherly bond like brothers. One will call and ask, "you got them?" and the other will respond, "yeah, I got 'em." It is so very interesting with the dynamics that can come out of these situations once you mature and allow those relationships to be built.

It has been amazing to see how things have come full circle. We still have our moments, but I think we are definitely in a good place. When you are able to kind of talk about things from the past and laugh about it, that helps. Of course, I think the one thing that I am mature enough to realize now is that when we talk about old things that happened, I try not to entertain the details. I have found the details is where the conflict is. In 2006 I remember it this way, but you remember it that way. The fact that you don't remember it my way is what's pissing me off and now we have an issue again. I do remember on one occasion explaining to the girls' mother that going back and rehashing the past sometimes is not worth the growth that you have made since then. It's just not worth the risk. If you saw it this way and I saw it that way....okay. Us really chopping through that and really breaking it down as to what happened is not worth risking where we are now.

GENERATIONAL TRAITS

The most important thing that I feel is something that I try to tell young fathers that I come across is being there. Money-wise I will say that my money has not always been where it needed to be. I actually told my oldest daughter's father on one occasion, "it doesn't cost for you to be in your child's life and that's all you have to do. The hardest thing was for me to stay in touch with my daughters when they were in Korea. That's when you have to put forth more of an effort. However, if you are just there, especially a man with female children everything else will work itself out. Now I'm not saying it's going to be peaches and cream. When I say be

143

there, like myself and one of my oldest buddies who is like a little brother, we went through a stretch where every weekend we played ball, and my youngest daughter was right there with me. Before that I would have her in a car seat on the side of the basketball court and when I was on the court the other fellas were watching her. I wasn't making separate bottles. I would get my big Nike water bottle and fill it up with Enfamil with iron and two water bottles. I would pack her bag like we were going to the gym. As long as she was with me that was the whole thing. I just needed her with me. It doesn't mean that you have to take the kids to Chuck E. Cheese every weekend and spend one hundred dollars. As far as clothing her, I did what I could, but the main thing is that she was with me.

I remember one summer I had one daughter playing AAU at the highest level and then her sister for her age group was doing the same thing. We didn't miss anything. No practices. No games. I would be in one City on one side of the County at a practice dropping one of them off, then driving all the way down to the opposite side of town or different county to see the other one play. That right there in itself, just by them looking up and seeing me in the stands and think "oh now I can ball out." It only cost me gas money and effort. You have to be there for your kids.

I don't remember a time when out all of the men in my life that somebody wasn't there for me. I don't recall that ever happening. So, that couldn't happen with my kids and my fellas were the same way. If for some reason I couldn't get there, then they showed up for my girls for me. All of them. We had and continue to have that village mentality. They were all also surrounded by men who were married and, in their kids,' lives as well. It was natural and now I have grown women who know that as a man you can't come at them incorrect because they know what a man is supposed to do and be like.

The traits that I feel I have carried from my parents' generation doesn't necessarily look the same. It may not be the exact road that I have followed but I have been able to create a support system. To watch my parents growing up, I too have been able to provide, support and encourage my children. They have no idea how much I sacrificed to do so. I was alone and still managed to provide the same things that a two-parent household would have done. So yes, I sacrificed a lot to ensure they had opportunities and anything else needed but the way that you sacrifice as a father, my children don't need to be privy to it. That's something that's hard as a single father but it needs to be done.

Whether you are a single mother or father it's still tough, but you have to do it. It's just the mentality that you have to find yourself in to be able be successful within it. You do what you are supposed to do as a parent. According to society, it's harder for a mother to do it than a father. Not taking anything away from any single mother ever because I have family and friends who have filled those roles. I learned from those single mothers around me in my circle. I saw them chose not to play the "woe is me" or the "damsel in distress' card. It was okay to play that card if they wanted to because it was in their deck. At any point in time, they could have played it, and someone would have stepped up and helped out.

As a single father you don't have that in your deck. If you try and play that type of card you will be looked at and possibly labeled as a weak individual or a dead-beat dad who is less of a man. That's one of the reasons you get cats out here selling or doing what they have to do in these streets to make ends meet in order to be there for their child because they can't play that card. If you do, then you are looked upon in a certain way. So, you just grin and bear it. There were even times that this whole single parenting situation got to me, and I was able to rebound. I can't imagine not having that support system yet still being required to do everything. Without that support system, who is there to tell that father that everything is okay, and they have his back. We got you. I know it's really tempting to go out here and make some fast money to buy your kid(s) some shoes, but you don't have to do that. How many men get to hear that? We either tighten up and handle our business or if you don't have that fortitude, you fold.

TODAY IN SOCIETY

I think society definitely does play a part in my children's' life. Even with them being six years apart, if you take a look at everything that has gone on just in the past three years alone. My youngest was in the class of 2020 and she was a part of the class that didn't get a graduation. Their basketball season stopped and then the world shut down two months later. Trying to get her through the whole thing of not having a prom or graduation and making the best of it was a task. She's an athlete so, the whole recruiting process, going to see colleges and stuff like that was different. She still ended up getting a scholarship and playing basketball, but it looked totally different as you envisioned it as a young athlete. You work all these years and then COVID affected that. Then she gets to school and it's her freshman year and the campus is pretty much shut down, and there's the mental health that came with that. To say that was really hard to deal with is an understatement. Especially as a father and you are watching your baby girl go through stuff and you don't know what to do.

Then at the same time that was happening we are faced with Black Lives Matter (BLM). It was interesting because that

146

was really when I felt that youngest one came out. She was for women's rights. She is a Marketing major and her whole goal is making sure that women have equal rights and equal opportunities in athletics. That's what drives her in college and is also what she wants to do in her career. So, yes, I think that society has affected her that way, as far as honing in on what she really wants to do.

The oldest one is different because she is here in the area. I'm watching her make the decisions that folks make in their late twenties. I'm trying to help her go through those things and get an understanding of how we are not saying things because we are your parents but because it's advice. The same stuff I went through myself.

I think that their mother and stepfather along with my significant other who I am currently with and myself remaining positive has been more of an influence than society. Because when they speak to anyone or when friends come over you will get and receive whatever either of the responsible adults say. Just as you do when you go to your mother's house. I think our ability to create this unit of adults that are all on the same team and rooting for them and they know that. We just want what is best for you guys. I think that has a greater effect on them.

These days there are so many negative images and influences that are out there for young women. Especially young Black women and they are going to get it regardless. They have their phones in their hands. They can entertain all of that but at the end of the day I find pride to hear my daughters say, "that's my dad," or "my dad doesn't go for that." They can tell all the dad jokes they want to tell but at the end of the day that's how I am.

I think that one of the biggest things that caused riffs in us is in my upbringing. I come from one area and there was a certain environment in which I was raised. She was coming from the City and that was a different environment in which she was raised. There was a point when I felt that our family needed to go to live in my home state. There was this image, this idea that I needed them to be raised the way that I was raised. Without me getting into the statistical stuff, I will just say that my argument was that the school system was much better in my home state than where we were in the City. What I couldn't take into consideration back then because I wasn't mature enough, was that I was asking her to uproot her life. I couldn't understand why there was resistance. To me it was a no brainer.

We are in the City and I'm trying to get us back across the water. For her, it was like, no I don't want to go. But, just like my stronghold was on my side, her stronghold was on her side. I think that if I had approached it differently, or if we had been able to communicate better, which wouldn't have happened because we just were not mature enough. That may have changed the outcome of things. Other than that, there's definitely some poor decisions that I made but, I am also where I am at right now because of those things. So, I can't be mad at the entire situation.

If there is anything that I could change, the hardest thing is the time that I lost with my daughters that I can't get back. I never saw my daughter's first day of school for first, second, or third grades. All of that was in Korea. When they returned back here and then left again, I had just built that relationship with my daughter. Basketball season was starting up in middle school. So, then it was seventh and eighth grades and then freshman and sophomore years of high school I wasn't there for that. My daughter tore her ACL and had a severe injury. I had never missed her play basketball until they moved. My other daughter started college and in her first year of college I couldn't be there for that. Those are moments that I will never get back. Regardless of how good we are or how far we've moved on, those are just moments in my children's life that I didn't experience because they weren't here. People used to tell me I could have flown out there. Yes, I could have but I am not talking about for that day or for a couple of days. I'm talking about your whole freshman year and all of the things that are new to you and you go through as a young lady in high school or as a freshman in college. Those are moments that I just didn't get to experience and can never get back.

WORDS OF WISDOM

First and foremost, just be there for your kids. That in itself is worth more than you realize. You will see the rewards of it down the road. If you were not raised to put God first, that's fine. Even if you are grown and don't understand the reason for it, you have got to find and make a way to have God in your kids' lives. Since I was raised in the church, there were relationships that were built, and I learned how to handle myself in certain situations. I do wish that I had my daughters more involved because there were some situations that they ended up going through in their teenage years and had they had that same 'church' in them that I had in me growing up, they would have been able to navigate through those issues better. That is no one's fault but my own. I could have easily gotten up every Sunday and taken them like I was made to do.

Be there and make sure that you have God in their life because it's those moments that they are not around, that spiritual upbringing is what's going to keep them from making those crazy decisions that their friends will make. I think every parent wants to have the kids in the car with their friends and know their child will say "either turn this car around or let me out."

Remember that every single decision that you make as a father will definitely have either a direct or indirect impact on your child. That's a fact.

"ALLEN"

GROWING UP

I always thought that I grew up with both of my parents in the household. However, as I got older, I discovered that the man I always called "Dad" was my stepdad, whom I carry his name. The funny thing is that I grew up with my "Dad," but my real father was my football coach. I have four siblings in all. My two sisters grew up with me in the same house where our mom and stepdad resided. My two sisters have the same biological set of parents. Then I also have two brothers, my birth father's sons by his wife. My brothers and I grew up knowing one another but not initially knowing we were brothers, but we thought we were cousins by marriage. I was the oldest of all the siblings, but we were all close. I do feel as if I had a wonderful childhood.

Growing up I thought I was rich. We didn't have a pot to piss in, but I thought we were rich. I used to consider McDonald's like a steakhouse. We felt it was the best thing we could ever have eaten when we ate it. That's why I always tell people they should be thankful for what they have. As long as you are breathing and able "to do," then you should be okay. My childhood overall was phenomenal. I never missed out on anything or went without. I didn't grow up around any real serious drama.

While I was in high school, I played basketball and was good at it. Once I started getting hit harder while playing football when I was younger, I decided that basketball would be more of my speed. It was a good decision because it became my absolute passion. I graduated from high school and chose not to attend college because I wouldn't say I liked school. However, what I know now, I should have gone. As for me and playing ball, I would have made it to the NBA had I chosen to pursue it.

I have been working with a company for the last thirty-three years. I plan to do three more years before I retire. I am trying to wait until our youngest gets into college and ensure she is established. Once she gets settled in, I will be ready to stop working. However, with the duties that I perform now at my job, I may stay longer as long as they don't mess with me. Once I do retire, I plan to stay at home doing nothing for a while. I do have some home projects that I plan on working on for the inside and outside of our home. The option of going back to training kids for basketball is always on the table for me to take up some of my time. My youngest brother and I will be able to train athletes in high school and prepare them for college sports. We have discussed it along with the goal of getting a warehouse and turning it into a training facility. Otherwise, if push comes to shove and I decide not to do anything, at least I know that I have been able to properly prepare for my future for my family to be straight.

All of my siblings get along well and are very tight knit. Our relationship is good, but it did take my sisters a little longer to accept my brothers. At first, they couldn't believe I wasn't their full-blood brother, and it took them a while to understand everything. I was the one that suffered through the pain of our family makeup. Back in the day, when moms didn't tell the kids who they really were until they found out, nobody wanted to say if it was true. Responses to questions were always like, "Did you ask your mom" or "Did you ask your dad." So, I had to do all of the research. When I asked my aunt, she didn't hesitate. She just said, "Yes, that's your father."

I was about seventeen or eighteen when I discovered my stepdad was not my biological father. I knew before, but it didn't start panning out or coming out until then. The funny thing was that my brothers and I all spent the night together. We used to spend the night over at one another's houses. They knew, but I think they didn't say anything to me because somebody told them that.

My mom, my stepdad (remember I am named after him), my biological dad, and his wife all grew up in the same neighborhood. At one time, they were all pretty good friends and would hang out together. From the bits and pieces that were told to me and what I had to figure out, it appears that back then, one of the couples split up, and then two of the individuals from each couple started seeing one another. My stepfather went into the military and started dating another woman. Upon that relationship ending, he returned to the area, and at the time, my mom was in a relationship with my biological dad when she ended up pregnant. Realizing then that she was still in love with my "stepfather," she rekindled the relationship with him.

My stepfather was an upfront and 'real dude.' Had I gotten the opportunity to ask him about the situation before he passed when I was fourteen, he would have told me the truth. But, as I said, this only came out once I was at least seventeen years old. I do remember him and my mom having some issues as I was growing up. Those issues had a lot to do with that. That's just my personal opinion. Now, in hindsight, I can picture what happened when I look back and visualize some incidents. Through all of that, it made me a better person.

When everything came out about my football coach being my biological father, it was different, but it wasn't. He always accepted me as a son but not a physical son. I would always have to call him, and he would say he was coming to see my kids. Then he wouldn't show up. There was always an excuse for something coming up. Whatever the case may be, I understand that people have their own lives. I get it. We would sometimes talk on the phone for about an hour or two. I accepted that. When I saw him, we would get along and laugh together. My brothers would try to make me get more into it, but I would tell them "No. I'm the victim; I'm the child. I don't have to make up for anything. I didn't ask to be here; they created me. They should try to get me to a point where I understand what is happening. I'm finding out all this stuff on my own." There were a number of major events in my life that he didn't show up for. That's a whole different story.

GENERATIONAL TRAITS

I had a terrific relationship with my stepfather. He was my main man and was always there for me. However, everyone has their shortcomings, and his was the use of substances. The battle of drinking and drugs that we see people having to deal with and how it brings a lot of things out of people. I'm sure it made him, and my mother's marriage plagued with problems. My mom, being the soft-spoken woman she is, has always been the woman that whomever she is involved with, she is into them more than 100 percent. No matter what the situation is. As a housewife back then, she didn't have the confidence level to take on the mindsight of "I don't need to be abused by you." Her heart and soul made her want to hang in there and work things out with my stepfather.

There were times when we, the kids, had to stop them from arguing. They would stop most of the time. Then, we would return to our state of being a happy family. I don't know if anything was done to her after the fact, if he did anything to her, or if they argued when we were not around, but our normalcy would return. We grew up in an era when arguments were the norm. The kids would hear them and say to one another, "Oh, they are going at it again." After a while, it would be over. I never saw any physical abuse. That was good, though, for me. It helped me not to see anything like that growing up because I did pick up not to hit or abuse a woman. Physically or verbally.

Watching and hearing them was a big life lesson for me. It taught me to pause. When I am upset now, that is what I do. I have learned early to know that there is no middle for me. It is that I am either happy or I'm gone off the edge. So, to eliminate any of the latter, I pause, think about things, and do my best to calm the situation down. That's what I could pick up from my childhood, which has helped me immensely.

I also learned from my stepfather to take care of my family by any means necessary. I saw him always ensuring that we never went hungry as a family. He always made sure that we had clothes on our backs. No matter what type of situations he and my mom may have gone through, my stepfather ensured that we saw him at the correct times. During the times when any of us may have been down or hurt, he was there. He taught me a lot of valuable life lessons. He showed me how I should look like a man. He taught me how to present myself to a grown-up with respect. We had to say, 'Yes ma'am' or 'Yes sir,' and there was no getting around it.

I have thought about the difference in raising kids now versus back then. For instance, when we were growing up, we couldn't even walk down the street and curse. Your adult neighbor would see or hear you and tell you to "come here and lemme slap you in the mouth." Then let you know that they were going to tell your mom why they slapped you so you could get it when you got home too. At that point, you already knew that you were going to be in trouble because you knew your mom didn't want anyone talking badly about their kids. It was a different world back then.

I do now, if I see young guys on the street or if I just pass them in the store, I will speak to them first. I like to know what their demeanor is when I say something. Even if they mean mug me or give me a bad look or say something crazy, I'll just say something like "hold up young fella I just want to speak to you for a second. I would like to know what's your future like. Do you want a job? Do you want a future for your kids, for your family? Anything. The hustle is real out here." That's how I will get the conversation started and they'll ease up. Real quick. Then they will be like 'oh, this is a real guy; like he is a real dude.' Sometimes they will have a look on their face as if they are thinking 'Nobody ever just came up to me like that.' I love it every time I can get them. A lot of times they may respond with "nah, I'm good.' Or something like that. I just want them to understand that everybody isn't after them, and everybody is not mean. You know what I mean. I want them to realize that some good people are still out here.

MEMORIES

My most negative memory that has impacted me from my childhood into my adulthood was seeing my stepdad shoot up, to find him unconscious and never coming back. That was the hardest thing that I have seen and been through as a child. I sat there and called his name over and over. I tried to get him up. I had to call my neighbors, and we were walking around trying to get him back and trying to revive him. The whole neighborhood came out to see what was going on and see if they could help. It was like it just shut down and stopped the entire community. It messed everybody up. It was a very sad day. It was almost like the Len Bias story because he was a neighborhood guy. He was the father figure that would take all of the kids in the neighborhood riding around on his motorcycle. He used to have four or five kids riding with him. On any given day, he may have one on his shoulder, three on the back, and one on the front. Just riding them around and showing them a good time. All the kids loved him of course. Most of the kids around did not have a father in their household or in their life. So, they enjoyed those times with him tremendously.

So that day was one of the hardest things for me to see at the age of fourteen because that was actually the second time. The first time I did not see him shoot up, but I knew that he was because we found the stuff. It was a day when the family was over at my aunt's house for a cookout. My dad stated he was going home for a minute. After a while, my mom tells me, "Your dad isn't back; what is he doing?" So, I decided I would go and check on him. I get to the house, and I can see through the window that he is in the kitchen sitting in the chair slumped over.

I ran back to the cookout and told my mom what I saw and that I was banging on the door with no answer. My uncle and cousin ran across to our house, and I ended up going back and climbing through our bedroom window to get to the kitchen and try to wake him up. At that time, I see all of these puddles on the kitchen floor and almost slip trying to get to him. I made it to the door and opened it for my uncle. He came in and as soon as he saw my dad, he just said, "d**n." Not knowing this as a child I thought he had spilled something. What I found out is that means he was already gone at that point because everything in his body had come up. We get him up and try to walk him around and see if he will wake up and try to get him to the point where he is okay.

For this to happen a second time and he does not survive was disheartening for me. To see the ambulance there and have the paramedics come out after about fifteen minutes and say he wasn't going to be here anymore and that he was gone was difficult. In my head, I remember seeing him go through this before, so I just knew he was going to pull through. To not be able to say, "I love you Dad" for the last time was super hard. I think that if he had been sick and was expected to not survive, it would have been a little easier for me because, at that point, he was supposed to have been clean from drugs. He had promised me that he wasn't going to do it anymore. I didn't want to accept it. I was waiting for him to be okay so I could find my rage about it and tell him what I was feeling. That's all that I can remember about that day. That day will forever be with me.

My most positive memory as a child was me playing sports. Everybody in my family used to come out and see me play. It was a great time but after my Dad passed, no one came to see or support me. Before then everyone used to come out and watch me play football because I was good at it. They used to come, and I would see them hoopin' and hollerin' on the sidelines those were joyous memories.

It was good to have everyone together on any occasion. We had a big family and used to have family reunions all the time. Being family oriented is deep down inside of me. Even to this day I am always striving to get the family together to keep that tradition going. Everyone that knows me understands how much my family means to me. I am more of a giver than a taker. Like on Christmas when my kids ask me what I want, I tell them I don't want anything. I just want them all here for the holiday and make sure that they are opening gifts. That makes me happy because that's my gift. I don't have anything that I want. If you want to give me something that is okay, but I am happy just watching them be happy.

I was already married, and we had been together for about six months, but things were not going as planned so we separated. We stayed apart for about two years until we ended up back together. That is when I found out I was going to be a father. I was twenty-two years old. I was excited because I always wanted to have kids, but she didn't. We ended up buying a home and then my daughter was born first then later my son. Our marriage still was not one that made both of us happy, so after not being able to take it any longer, I decided to leave. It was better for me to be separated than for me to be in the same household with a toxic relationship.

Upon me leaving the house that I left for my wife and two children, we had to settle into a new way of living. We had to learn to co-parent with one another to ensure that our two children were able to get the most from the both of us. During that time, we agreed that due to our inability to maintain a healthy relationship within our home we would divorce.

I eventually started dating another woman who had two children of her own. From day one, her oldest, her son's father and I have been cool. I had already known him for years as he was growing up yet what I didn't know was that he was the father of this woman's son. However, since we already knew one another from a distance, we were able to remain on good terms with one another concerning any type of co-parenting. We are all able to get along with no real issues. He is able to come to my house and we sit around and chat and have a good time.

However, everything doesn't always fit in a puzzle like we would like it too. Her daughter's father was a completely different story. What I will say about that situation is this;

just don't lie to the kids. That's one of my biggest pet peeves. If you can't make it, then say you had to work late or you had to do something. Don't just not show up at all after you have told the child that you are coming. I would rather you give an excuse to a child than have nothing at all to say. Don't make promises to a kid that you are coming, and they are waiting at the door for you, and you never show up. Then you call the very next day and say you are coming on that day. At that point is when I have to step in and say, "no you are not." I can't stand around and watch a child have to go through that. Now, when she got to a certain age and it was still happening, and she was able to say she wasn't going or didn't want to go, because 'her Dad' (meaning me) is right here. It was like that for years and has been so ever since.

My current wife and I have been married for almost twenty years. We have one daughter together. So, within our blended family, we do not have his and her children, but we have a total of two sons and three daughters. There is never any type of 'step' or 'half' brothers or sisters in our household. They tell everyone, 'That's my brother; that's my sister,' and they don't say anything else. There was a short span of time when my oldest daughter was having a little difficulty with the change and additions to the family because of her loyalty to her mom. After a while, she did come around and fell in love with my wife just as much as I had. Eventually, she and my son had to go to their mom and communicate their feelings to her. They had to tell their mom that they both loved and cared for my wife.

It took a while for my ex-wife to really get to know my current wife for herself. Even though our two children had provided her with their declaration of love for her, she was still hesitant. It was on one occasion when we all had to come together for a family celebration and my ex-wife was able to fully see over a span of consecutive days how my current wife interacted with my oldest son and daughter. This in itself helped her to see things a bit clearer and the bonds between them started to grow. I think this particular event has really shared a big light between the two of them in order for there to be a meeting of the minds and hearts for the betterment of the entire situation.

Amidst all of the silent allegations and assumptions of who did what to who and why between my ex and myself, I remained silent. I continued to strive and start fresh, just focusing on rebuilding myself and at the same time not allowing what I was going through to have a negative impact on my children. I let things play out as I saw fit, and my truth came to light eventually. It wasn't until years later that some individuals did approach me and apologize for their behaviors and lack of support toward me. Had I taken the time years ago to explain to individuals about what happened within my first marriage, most of them would not have believed what I was saying. It is in times like this that being true to yourself and what you know to be right that the naysayers will see the truth in any situation.

I look back now, and I cannot even think of any one time that there were issues regarding us co-parenting. When my children would come and visit me, they knew they were in the midst of a well-rounded, loving, and welcoming home. They were always excited to come visit and spend time with me. One thing that I can say is that I have been blessed through it all by not having to spin my wheels, proving to my children that I am or could be a great dad. I just did what I knew to do, and it showed up in them naturally. Even though I may have been going through emotional and financial issues involving their mother, our children knew from my actions what my stance was throughout it all.

Looking at what my steps in life have afforded me as far as opportunities, I can see the whole concept of each one teach one. My oldest bonus son is now a father, and I can see how he has and continues to mirror what he has seen me do through the years. He fully understands that being with a woman means that you have to treat her like the queen that she is. I have also made sure that should things not work out between the two of them, that he must remain relevant in his child's life in order to be a great father. I explained to him that I have already been through those channels for you and that he does not have to be engulfed in misery. Just make sure that you are doing the right thing for both of them at all times.

I have always had a good support system while the kids were growing up. My sister loved my kids, and they would go over there almost every other weekend. She didn't care because she just wanted to see the kids. My oldest son's grandmother was a great asset to us as well. In fact, she kept me and my wife's child when she was a baby. It was just an easy fix for us. She would just come over to our house every morning to watch the baby for us. It didn't matter that this baby did not have her blood flowing through her; she already knew that we all were a family. An all-inclusive family. It goes without saying that our youngest daughter understands now that she has three grandmothers. No questions from her as to why or how. To this day, this woman who has been there for her will always be her grandmother.

DO OVER

I was struggling with myself. It was harder for me at certain points to not contribute to what they really needed at certain times. To this day, I beat myself up about that. Like there were times that maybe I didn't feel like going outside that day with them. If I had gone outside with them and not done anything but just be there, it would have far outweighed me not going outside with them at all. That kind of messed with me a lot. To this day, I have found myself repeating that cycle with my youngest daughter and playing basketball when she wants to go outside and train. I find myself saying "I don't feel like going." Then I will reflect back on it and realize that I can't do that because I will be right back in the same trap. So, I have made a big effort to change that behavior on my part. It's not that I don't want to be a part. It's just by the time I come home from working outside all day it gets to be a little overwhelming. However, in order to change things, you have to change yourself first. So now if she says she wants to watch a Marvel movie I am right there beside her (even though I may not have a clue what's going on in the move), I'm there.

If I had an opportunity to do things differently from the beginning. I would have taken the time in my life to wait and weigh things out before allowing myself to become a parent. I believe with what my wife and I have been able to pour into all of our children (hers, mine, and ours), and a number of obstacles that I faced early on in parenting could have been avoided.

When you have a partner who is truly in love with you emotionally and physically, they go to bat for you. There is nothing that anyone can say to or against you that they won't show up for. Anything that is not right with me or anyone that goes against me, including the kids, she is there for me. I had never experienced anything like that until I started dating my wife. For someone to say and show how much they love me in everything they do is something I could have ever imagined would be a part of my life. She loved me when I didn't have anything at all. I used to come home for about three months with a paycheck that would have fifty dollars leftover, and my wife was right there with me. Her words ring in my ear and my heart to this day. She just said, "I gotchu" and I didn't need anything else. That's the kind of love and support that I wished that I had from the beginning. To pour into me while she stood beside me and sometimes in front of me leading me.

Looking at the values of family and being around other kids, whose families have been torn apart. Things like absent parents, or lack of affection toward one another or showing emotions. Those are a number of things that we hear from a lot of kids. My wife and I have gone to different schools for our children only to have other kids come up to us and ask if they can come to our house for the weekend or can we do this with you and more. We have even had other kids come up to us telling us 'our parents don't act like y'all do.' Over the years we have taken in at least five other kids that had at some point been thrown out of their homes for one reason or another. Some of these same kids still come by to visit to this day and see about us. Whether it is to see if we are in need of anything or just to love on us in general.

It's a beautiful thing to see. To have these kids flourish into young adults and have them come back and tell us what it meant for them to have someone like us in their corner in times of need. It's things like this along with seeing all of my children doing what they want to do in their lives and prospering within it that lets me know that I am blessed. I can't ask for anything more. I can't ask for anything to be any different. Especially with my boys and not getting into any trouble. I am not saying that they were innocent because I know they have done some dirty stuff. They already knew from early on if they were doing drugs or something illegal that they would be on their own and not to bring any of that across my doorstep. It's just a blessing that they snapped out of it and wanted to do well.

WORDS OF WISDOM

The first thing I would say to a young man coming behind me is that always remember that a child did not ask to be here. The parent of a child is that child's superhero. So, everything that kids know and does is because of one of you, if not both. It's important if you want your child to be something in life, to grow as a young man or young lady you have to be in their life. I don't care if you never had the chance to be what you wanted to be. Like I always tell my kids.....be better than me. I want you to be more successful than I was. Even though I did the things that I could do for you all, I want you to be better than that.

The hardest thing in a child's life is to have a parent that doesn't understand what's right and wrong. Most kids don't know what's right or wrong because they are not being taught. You have to teach your child everything the right way. Whether it's 'yes ma'am' or 'yes sir' or even a simple yes. Instead of saying 'what' because that word is really ugly when you get it as a response after asking a question. I tell people if you say 'what did you say' I'll respect that. But if you just say 'what' that means I got on your nerves at some point as if I am irritating you. Most people have no understanding of how powerful that one four letter word is when it is used as a response to a call. You have to show your kids how to give respect in order to get it. You don't have to be a thug to earn respect. You don't have to be a knucklehead to earn respect. You can be a great person to earn respect. Show love to have respect. Apologize to have respect. Admit that you're wrong to have respect.

It's a lot of things that you can show a kid in your daily walk that is not bad. You can show them how to react to situations that are bad. Kids see and take in whatever their parents bring to the table. My sons gloat on me a lot because I showed them how to be a man. Not so much as to learn how to fight or protect themselves (which I did do) but they gloat on the fact that I have shown them how to be a family man. They say that I showed them what life is all about and it is okay to not want to be poor or to just settle. I have taught them how to do things for themselves because with me I try not to ever have to go to someone to ask for anything. If I ever have to then you already know because of who I am that I have already tried any and everything to accomplish why I am coming to you.

You don't have to walk around wearing your pants down and showing that you wear droopy drawls. That's not showing anyone that you know how to be a man. If I was a businessman and approached by a guy with saggy pants showing his underwear, I am not going to give him the time of day because the first thing he is showing me is that he doesn't care about himself or his appearance as a grown man. The possibility of having a conversation or an open-door opportunity starts with that. If you walk up to someone with a rugged appearance, then the conversation more than likely won't even get started. However, if you approach someone in just the opposite manner with your clothes pulled up and speaking with grammar that requires an adult convo then that person will more than likely be open to it.

It doesn't matter if you have been to jail fifteen times and you have a child, you have to switch things up. There is nothing like being involved in a child's life and showing him your behaviors and lifestyle and then years later when they have followed your footsteps verbatim you can't for the life of you figure out what happened. Yes, you may have been in your child's life but the blueprint that you laid down for them is what they learned from. You as a parent usually do not know how badly your child wants to be like you. So, if you want them to be different then it starts with you as a man.

"Tume"

GROWING UP

I was born in a small town in the South. I come from a very large family. My mother gave birth to fifteen children, and I am number twelve out of all my siblings. All of us didn't live together in the same house at the same time but as many as ten of us did. I had a happy childhood, as far as not really having any big responsibilities other than to try and be a happy kid. It was sad in the fact that we couldn't afford some of the things that other children had because we were very poor. However, my mother made being poor not a bad thing by her nurturing. So, as a child, I was poor, but I was blessed.

I don't have any bad memories as a child. We lived on eighty-five acres at the time that my family owned. This property has been in my family since the early 1800's. My great grandfather, who was a former slave, acquired the property which was a sawmill where he worked. I guess that was one of the things that we had an advantage of. Back then the Black community owned a lot of their land even though it may have been desolate. Our land was "farmland" because that is what my great-grandfather did to provide and make a living from. He raised my mother and her five sisters. Once he passed on, my mother took over the property and that is where we were raised. As kids we played outside and did gardening. Those were my fun times. Even though I was poor; we were happy.

Initially, my siblings and I had both parents in the household. At some point between me being six and seven years of age, my parents separated. That is when my mother pretty much raised all of us.

In going back over our complete family makeup, I do need to state that my father had five other children from a previous marriage. They are much older than me, so I didn't grow up with them. My oldest siblings from my mom grew up with them. He had five from that marriage and then five with my mother.

Due to my parents' tumultuous relationship, the purpose or intent of my parents' separation was to not have my father involved in the upbringing of us as a unit. Once it occurred, I didn't see my father anymore until I was an adult. I know for a fact that my siblings that were in my age group did not have any type of contact with him. I can't be so sure about my older group of siblings and him. I believe it was around the time that I got out of the military that I had any type of contact with him.

As I was growing up, my biggest influences were my older brothers. I guess I can say that they kind of stepped in where my father was not in regard to what one might call "rites of passages." My mom was a strong woman. Not just strong in the sense of physical strength but in the aspect of being able to push through and get things done. She was deaf from the time she was nine years old. She could not hear what was going on, but she was always a part of everything. She raised fifteen kids as a deaf person. She was born in 1922, so you can imagine what the times were like, especially in the South. As difficult as it was, she made sure that she was there for us and instilled in us the best she saw fit.

My oldest brother took the lead as far as being the "head male" of the family. Actually, he was the one who I like to use the term "rescued us" from the situation with my father. He helped us to leave our original home to move to another state where he was residing. I had five older brothers. They didn't live with us, but they constantly checked in to see how we were doing. There was one that did live with us, did so until he was eighteen or nineteen and it was at that point that he started branching out on his own.

My mother did date other men and I don't have any bad recollection of anyone. They were strong men and they accepted all of us kids along with my mother. I never felt mistreated or abused by anyone that my mother dated. They always supported us. One of the men was my youngest sister's father. She was the only child that my mother had with someone other than my biological father. My sister's father was with us all the way up until his passing and we have always considered him to be a part of the family.

With my biological father not being present in my life as I was growing up, it left something to be desired. At the time you are going through it, you don't understand it. Once you are able to reflect on it as you are becoming an adult you realize the absence of your father has left some residual stuff within you. I remember when I was in the military and laying up in my bunk thinking about why I never had a relationship with my father. I used to hear guys talking about some of the things that their fathers had told and showed them. Yet I had no recollection of anything along those lines. I kind of felt resentment at that point because I felt like he cheated me out of something.

I think the biggest thing that hurt me was to see my mother go through what she went through as a single parent. I think that probably hurt me more than anything that my father did or didn't do. Him abandoning my mother was probably something I never got over. In all actuality from the time, we left our home state, up until the day he passed, I was still disturbed about it. When it was time to attend his funeral, I didn't even feel like I was a part of it. I couldn't figure out how they were expecting me to grieve over a person that I didn't even know. I had a very large disconnect with him. People say, I need to get over it, but it is something that any child or adult can do; you just don't get over it. You put it to the side but at different moments of your life it comes back to you.

Once you start having children, it's then that you find out that you don't have anything from your father to impart into your child. That was probably the biggest thing I dealt with once I started having children. Even though I had all girls, I couldn't say to them that this is a childhood memory from me and my father. I could only say. "these are memories from me and my mother." To this day, I tell people all the time when they ask me, "I can't tell you one thing that my father taught me." That was simply because there wasn't anything.

That causes a void and resentment in men. You see what happened with my mother is still happening to women today. Not just African American families. For the most part it is in our communities that the man leaves the household, and he leaves the woman responsible for everything that he leaves behind. The mother is left to mend the child's heart as well as her own. Those are the types of things that I believe are causing a lot of young men to have resentment once they grow up. They have not been shown from a man's point of view how to handle things.

Now this didn't happen to me because I was not raised in or by the streets. I did fortunately get a different set of morals and values instilled in me through my mother and my brothers. We didn't live in what the kids call now, "the hood." We lived in the country down South where everything had a value. Today because of the missing fathers, oftentimes nothing has a value to it. A number of them don't understand the value of creating a child and end up with the mindset of allowing "the system" to take care of that child. Now, this is not all of the time but a number of us have witnessed this to be true at some point in our lives. This generally happens because that parent did not have the guidance that he needed when he was growing up.

When you come up without the aid of a father or a father figure, you do tend to feel slighted. So, when it was time for you to become a father and you yourself did not have your own father to show you the ropes. What are you yourself as a father going to pour into your child? This is why a lot of father's end up not pouring into their kids from experience or lessons taught. They use their hard life lessons and that is generally not enough to rear a child and be successful at it. That is kind of what happened to me. Not from a street mentality but nothing from my father's side to bring to the table but all from my mother's side. If someone is not teaching you right from wrong, then you better believe that wrong is going to come first before right if you are in the streets. When you are in the streets then it's like crabs in a bucket. Everybody is trying to survive, and nobody has the proper tools for survival.

Oftentimes when you see that, especially in a group, the majority of them were not raised by a real man. So, these guys are making decisions by calling themselves a man. You have thirteen-year-olds out here thinking they are grown. Just because they have been left to make these decisions on their own. Whether they want to be grown or not, when you left them as their father, that is the position that you left for them to be in. Survival is like a primitive instinct. Whether you do right or wrong, the decisions that you tend to make are made off of pure survival mode. The bottom line is that a father not being in the house definitely causes a lot of issues. Particularly with young men. However, this does not exclude young ladies because girls need their father in their

175

life just as much as a boy does. So, when we as men walk away from our children, we are not making decisions on our knowledge because it was never taught to us.

I did not finish high school. However, once I went into the military it was something that they stressed very much. So, while I was in the Army, I obtained my GED and went on to attend college while I enlisted. As I have stated, when I was young, we lived on a farm, so education was secondary. For us, being able to eat and pay bills was primary. My brother and I would trade places often. We would go to school one day and then go to the field and work the next. We'd go to school maybe three days a week and work the other four days out of the week. So having the opportunity while in the Army, I did get to go a little further in my education with completing just short of my two-year degree.

My occupation in my youth was as a farmer up until about 1977 when I was a soldier. In 1975 I started driving a truck which opened the door for my military entrance, and I was a soldier for about six years. After leaving, I had the basic thoughts that a number of soldiers did. I just knew I was going to become a civilian and work at a desk. Yet, I had already fallen in love with the transportation field. I continued to drive for years and just retired about three years ago. It has benefited me quite well. I don't have any qualms about it, and I call myself lucky because transportation has allowed me to live the life I live now as opposed to the life I lived as a child. When I was growing up, I always wanted or needed something but as an adult I don't want or need anything. Being able to reap the benefits of something that I started doing when I was a young man, has afforded me and my family multiple opportunities to live life to the fullest. Transportation is my industry and has led me to this position that I am able to live in today. I am settled into retirement, but I do have my hands in co-ownership of a company. I do the behind-the-scenes activity because the actual road trips are a little bit more than what I would like to do. It was enjoyable at the time but now I'm just enjoying life to the best of my abilities. God has blessed me in the aspect of my kids have not had to go through or endure any of the issues that I have mentioned that I had to go through growing up.

MEMORIES

My most negative thoughts from my childhood that have impacted me is my own father. He wasn't what I consider a man. I didn't know that as a kid because I looked at him as my father. Once I became a man and realized the qualities of a man, I remembered never seeing those qualities in my father. The most negative thing in my life is that my father never showed me that he was a man. He showed me what not to be. Having a drunken father was probably my most negative childhood memory. All my other memories of once we left my father when I was about six or seven have all been positive. They were hard but they have been positive experiences. The only times that I felt sad was when my mother was with my father because I know that he would work all week, make bootleg liquor, 'the man' would take it all from him, and my father would go to the juke joint and then stumble home on Sunday completely broke with ten children in the house and no food. That went on up until we left. That was one of the reasons my mother left him, because he just never amounted to anything.

My baby sister's father came into our lives about 1965 when I was about eight or nine years old. He kind of was like as I present myself as. Even though we never called him dad or anything like that, he treated us just as if we were his. I remember when I was in the seventh grade, and they still had corporal punishment in school. This boy and I skipped class and went outside of the school compound and on our way back we met the principal. Of course, back then, he wanted to proceed with beating me and I told him he was not going to put his hands on me. I went home and told my mother what happened and of course she said, "no ain't no white man putting his hands on you." So, my mother told my sister's dad about the incident and unbeknownst to me when I returned to school the next day the principal called me to his office. I guess he figured he would give me his punishment that I stopped him from doing the previous day. We didn't have a telephone or anything like that but just so happened, as I was walking into the school office I looked up and here comes my stepfather. He walked into the office, grabbed this guy, and grabbed him up by his collar and lifted him out of his chair. He looked him in the eyes and told him, 'you put your hands on my son, I'm putting my hands on you.' That was the greatest display of love someone had shown me outside of my mother that I had ever witnessed. I have never forgotten that to this day. The principal of course threatened to call the police and my stepfather says, 'call them because if he puts his hands on my child then I'm gonna do the same thing to him.' My stepfather did what he felt the need to do as a father. I remember him later on telling all of us, 'if y'all get into any trouble, make it home and we'll take care of the trouble.'

That was my most positive memory and that comes from what most would call a "step" parent. However, when you get involved in a child's life and show them love, understanding, compassion and the things they need to grow then they do just that. Grow and respect you so much that it doesn't really matter if you are their real father or not. They know that they can always come to you. That has been my blueprint in life. I'm not your father but I will do father-like things and want you to know that you can count on me. If they want to take it to their biological father, then I'm still there and will be happy to co-anchor that with him. It's all about making the child feel secure.

BECOMING A FATHER

This is a trick question for me to start at the beginning. I was actually eighteen years old when I became a father. However, I was not aware of it. I met my oldest child when she turned thirty-six years old. It really hurt me that I didn't find out until years later and to this day I still don't have a concrete reason. My daughter's aunt was married to my brother. The woman that raised my daughter was my brother's wife. I have been told that my daughter's aunt/mother raised her and made everyone keep the information tucked away once the biological mother passed away about a year after I went into the military. It was said that her mom didn't want me to know because she "felt that I wasn't going to be nothing." Without any deep and intellectual words to make it look pretty, I will just say that I had a one-time encounter with a young lady. I know that it only takes one time. However, I never had any other dealings with this young lady again because I was actually supposed to be dating her younger sister when this happened. In an effort from a young man's mindset, I opted to have sexual relations with the older sister instead of the younger sister who I was dating who was not sexually active. Then years later, thirty-six to be exact, my daughter found me. Everyone in the community knew one another and it was just kept a secret.

Fortunately, we have been in one another's lives for the last eleven years now. It is still a work in progress as everyone continues to learn from one another and adjust to this. We make every attempt to be all inclusive in family outings and activities to try and keep a continuity of growth.

During my first marriage, I did not have any children born of that union.

In talking about my first child that I knew about, it was kind of a planned thing. Remembering my background and how I grew up, I did not want to have a child and plop them down in the middle of a situation that was similar to that one. So, I waited and once I got into the military, I said I was going to give myself five years to build some type of career and being able to support a child. I had decided that I would plan to have a child when I was twenty-five years old. When I got to the age of twenty-two to twenty-three years old, I started to plan it out. Then, as I hoped, my child came one month before my twenty-fifth birthday. I was married (for the second time) and wanted to just start my own family. That was just one of the premises. I did not want to bring a child into this life until I had a life of my own set up because of what I had been through myself. I was in the military and in Germany at the time that she was born but it was a good experience. It was what my wife at the time and I had planned together. We ended up having another child from our union. We were married from 1980 until 1986.

Unfortunately, life came at me, and it got in the way of me parenting. I realized that I had the same problem that my father had, which was drinking. With my heavy drinking, I paid the ultimate sacrifice. I lost my career in the military and lost somebody that I really loved. We were both soldiers and we came back to the United States before our second child was born, I was told by my second wife that she had re-enlisted in the Army and she wanted to make a career out of it. Since I had just been released from the Army, I had no intention of being her spouse. My big idea was 'let me divorce you.' So, I divorced her and my children at the same time. I did the same thing that my father did. It haunted me for a long time. I spent seven years not being a part of my children's lives. I hurt the whole seven years. The one thing that I do thank God for is that the whole seven years, He put that weight on my shoulders that I'm not being a father. I was paying child support, but I wasn't supporting the children. I was there financially but not emotionally. Through good graces that changed in 1992 and since that day I have been an intricate part of their life.

My children were ecstatic about me re-entering their life. I guess they probably felt the same way that I did when I was younger, that I probably didn't love them. I'm sure they wanted to know why I wasn't there supporting them when they were young. We had to work through that because when I got back into their lives they were hurt. All I had been to them was child support paying daddy not a father that went to school plays and went to this event or that function. By my ex being in the military, she was always stationed where I was not. It wasn't util I got to the point where I finally realized that it wasn't her responsibility; it's my responsibility to be in my children's life. Once that kicked in, it didn't matter where they were at, I didn't have that as an excuse anymore. I started being a full-time father. That alone gave me the opportunity of getting the benefits of a full-time father. That is inclusive of the love and respect from my children.

It was during my third marriage that I feel as if God was punishing me. As I always say, our union was not of God and He had already told me what my problem was, but I just didn't want to believe him. I already had two previously failed marriages, so I was determined to make this one work. God had given me all of the signs showing that she and I were unequally yoked but I kept on ignoring them. So, I guess He had to show me. When I walked into the court room, my then wife entire demeanor changed. It was rough. I ended up abandoning my children as well as my principles.

I went and lived in the slums of another city, and this was totally out of my way of living. I lived there for seven years, and it was seven years of bad luck for me. During those years, I worked hard every day, yet I couldn't prosper. I have always had a job of some sort. At this time, I was a truck driver in the petroleum industry, making good money, but I could not find one ounce of success. The moment I left that situation in 1996, and came to where I am living now, my life skyrocketed. I was in the same field, doing the same job, but I was in a different environment. It was a healthier environment.

Moving forward (but backward). I met my current wife back in 1986. However, I was already married but legally separated at the time to another woman. So, I was living my free life or let's just call it the single life. So, my current wife and I kind of dated briefly during this time. She was coming out of a situation of being with her boyfriend who later became her husband. We dated during that time when we were both starting new lives for about a year and a half until 1988 when I moved away and met my third wife and married her in 1989 and we stayed together until 1996.

Once I was out of my third marriage, I returned back to the area in 1996. Then me and my current wife had a phone conversation, but we didn't connect with one another. Around 1997 a friend of mine that knew about our relationship from the '80's, brought her up and I explained that I had been looking for her. We ended up reconnecting in late 1997 and started officially dating in 1998. We dated for about three years and have been married since 2001 for twenty-two years.

My wife already had two children at the onset of our marriage. Our son (because I was definitely his father in every sense) was a special needs child and he passed on in

2022. When I originally met my current wife, I only knew of two children that were biologically mine at the time. Those were my two daughters, and they were not residing in the area. They were in a different state because their mom was still stationed elsewhere. However, my two daughters would come and visit, and I would introduce and include them with my new family. I don't know of any really bad situations between us.

The one instance I can recall is when I believe my stepdaughter was having her first child. My youngest daughter, who was in college and dating at the time, felt some kind of way. She believed that if I got too attached to my stepdaughter's child, that I wouldn't love her child as much. It caused a little riff, with my daughter winding up moving and relocating to another state. So, then my first grandchild was born in a different state as opposed to being near family. It created chaos but it was eventually talked about and worked out and time healed wounds. Having a blended family has been pretty much a blessing to me.

What I would like to touch on at this time is when you are dating a woman and she has children. If I really care for her then I want to accept the children along with her. I don't believe in using the word 'step' concerning children. The word is only used when someone else says it to me. All of the children from the relationships I have been in along with my biological children are all my children. No prefixes are ever used by me to address or describe them. When asked, "how is your stepdaughter/stepson doing?" I always respond with "my daughter/son is fine." Because of the love that men that dated my mother showed me when I was growing up, I automatically give that same type of love to those children that I am around.

So, with my son (stepson), when I met him, he was differently abled but that just made me love him more not less. I realized that he couldn't do anything about his situation, and he had to depend on other people to survive. What mostly struck me with my son was that he was so covered by God that I had to get through God to get to him. He was totally covered and blessed.

When I first met him and started coming around, his mother used to puree his food. We had been dating for a little while, his grandmother used to come and get him and take him to school. Well because of who I am, I didn't want him to be around everyone and wanted myself to get in the circle of being around him. I vigorously tried to get into the lives of both him and his sister. He wasn't vocal and couldn't tell me what he did or did not want or like, but his older sister was very vocal about how she felt. However, the covenant that he had with God, before I could even walk into his room, I had to have a big smile on my heart as well as on my face. That was the only way that I could approach him. Once I learned to do that, we fell so in love with one another. It got to the point that my wife would leave me home with just him and I had never had any experience of taking care of a special needs child before. Eventually, I found myself thinking, "hell I can do this better than you."

Even though he couldn't walk, stand, or see, I would put him in the truck and let him feel what I was doing. I have an old car that I rebuilt as a hot rod, and I put him in there with me, but the noise was too much for him. So that was a no-go for us to spend time together but what I did was place a picture of him on the dash of the car. I have had the car for fifteen years and his picture has been there the entire time. Since he couldn't ride with me, I wanted to make sure his spirit was riding with me.

In the beginning you are raising somebody else's child. When opinions are not the favored opinion that a person is looking for, of course it comes up that 'you're not my dad.' Well, it's always been my thing of, hell no I'm not your daddy. I'm your provider. If in fact, I am your provider, then these are the things that I'm looking for in order for me to continue to provide for you. I'm looking for respect, understanding and I'm gonna give the same things that I'm looking for. I believe that is what helped to smooth out the wrinkles because I gave respect, guidance, and love. Then the next thing that I know, we are one big happy family.

Even with my current wife's sister's kids, I consider them mine. I take care of them. Although they are adults, I do what I can for them. Take for instance her (my) niece, I gave her away at her wedding because she didn't want her father to be involved. The other child stayed with her father for a number of years but now that she is back here, that leaves me to be the father of the bunch. Over the time that my niece was alone, I would always reach out to ask her if she needed anything. If she saw me making a delivery at a gas station, she would stop, and I would make sure that I would slip a little money in her pocket so that she would be alright. Even though she would never ask me for it. That's just the love that I had for them. I'm proud to say that never changed and now that I'm older they reciprocate. They ask me, "Uncle, do you need this or that?" So, I really feel blessed.

Losing anybody is really difficult. My wife's son or should I say my son has been nothing but a son to me. Even though I am not his biological father, you couldn't have told him that. He never knew that and I'm not saying that because his father didn't participate. When I first started coming around and seeing him, I just started to whittle my way into the picture because I wanted to be in front of his heart. I mourn him every day. I don't know if I can put my feelings into words correctly but it's like the greatest sense of loss that I've had to this day. I lost my mother a few years ago and of course I felt bad, but my mother was ninety-two years old, so I felt great about the time that God gave her. Yet, with my son, I would get off work and I would be dead tired. I told you before that prior to being able to walk into his room that you had to talk to God. I could walk in the house with minimal to no energy, take my shoes off, walk upstairs to go into my bedroom to change clothes. I would see his room first and I would say "hey man" and it wouldn't stop there, even with my dirty clothes on. He would cause me to stop and sit there and talk to him for five or ten minutes. During that short time frame, my whole energy level would change.

I had walked in the house a drained person and leave out of his room reinvigorated. I would go out in the yard after working a twelve-hour day and then spend another five hours outside. The reason that I know that it was him was because in 2020, when everyone got hit with COVID, I stopped going to the yard. Now this year was my first year actively doing the yard and my first year doing anything without him. I'm a country boy and have always loved the outside.

Now I am struggling, I can't explain it. I just don't have that inspiration without him. Losing my son, I've lost a part of me that I'll never get back. The only thing that I can say now, and I don't mean this in a gory way. I can't wait to be reunited with him again. My life has definitely not been the same. I'm not sad or discontented but my happiness level is just not like it was when I was responsible for him. I always felt 100% responsible for his well-being. I don't discount his mother being responsible for him nor his father being responsible for him. Yet, from the day that I met him, I knew that it was my duty to be responsible for him. I was proud of that responsibility.

Every vacation that we went on I made sure that he participated just like the rest of my kids did. If we went somewhere where there was a pool, then I would make sure there was a chair lift so that he could be lowered into the pool. If we went to the beach, then I would make sure that he had a big, wheeled chair that could be rolled through the sand. Even during the times when we had get together and everyone would be on the main level and my son would be upstairs in his room, I would take him downstairs (until my wife would tell me it was too loud). This was me making sure that he would feel included in everything.

Yes, so that has been a really great loss for me. I don't know if I will ever get past it. It's a sadness that will never go away. You just kind of tuck it away and learn to deal with it. I mean even in the afterlife; I have gone out to fancy up his grave site in an effort to continue to take care of him. I had to go bling out his resting place. Even in the last year of his passing I have gone into his untouched room and laid on his bed to either sleep or just feel his presence or even talk to him as if he were right there next to me. I will never let go of how I feel. Actually, I don't ever want to let it go. He was a sense of pride for everybody in this family.

I've shared with you that I have been married four times. A woman almost had to pull my teeth to get me to say 'I love you' but she doesn't have to do anything for me to demonstrate it. Even when my current wife now used to say, 'you didn't tell me you love me.' Then I would ask her if any of my actions showed you anything different? She would respond with, "no, your actions are like you are head over heels." Then that is what I go off because I can tell you something that could be a lie, but if I show you something then you are going to see with your own eyes.

The reason why I adopted that mindset was because when I was a kid, after my father would be abusive to my mother, he would then say, "I love you." It became impossible for me to tell a woman that I loved them because it meant to me what my father said to my mother. To me the question has always been, if you love me, then why are you always putting your hands on me? So, I would rather demonstrate my love to you so that you are not wondering if I love you. You can see that I love you. It was the same thing with my children. Once I started showing them the love then things started to ease up and fall into place at that point.

REGRETS OR DO OVERS

In my kids' life I missed some years when their mother and I separated, and they were in another country, and I was here in the U.S. I spent about maybe five or six years with no contact with them. That is my deepest regret and if I had something that I could do over then that would be the thing. Sometimes life grants us a do-over and sometimes it doesn't. Right now, because of the relationship that we have, I'm not feeling so much pressure about yesterday. Especially since today is so good. I feel bad about the breakup because not only did I break up with their mother, but I broke up with my children too and that's something that I shouldn't have done. It's okay when adults break up, but it isn't okay to break up with the kids because it's a lifetime commitment with them.

WORDS OF WISDOM

I want to help the next generation of fathers be better than my generation or what they see right now. I think it kind of falls on all of us to do whatever we can whenever we can to help a young man. A lot of them, particularly inner-city youth, are really struggling with this manhood or adulthood. All you have to do is turn the TV on and you see twelve- and thirteen-year-olds stealing cars and shooting people. All that comes from is that they don't have a father teaching them right from wrong. A lot of them have mothers who are so busy worrying about everything else in life including raising their other children. Therefore, when they get outside it's their friends and the streets that are raising them.

If you are a parent, then listen to your children. Don't dismiss what they say or how they feel. Be open and honest with them. There are a lot of times that we say a child is too young to understand. If we take the time to explain things to a child, then it helps them to grasp and puts them in a better place emotionally and mentally with some things that they may generally not understand. Then, that in itself, because you have taken the time to explain and talk things over with them, they will in turn, remember that. When the time comes that they need to confide in you, they will be more comfortable because you as the parent has already initiated some type of dialogue without shutting them out.

If both parents are around and involved in raising the child, you must remember that just because you have a child in common doesn't mean that you will automatically parent the exact same way. The mother may want to do things one way and you as the father may want to do something totally opposite. However, remember that the paramount thing here is that you have to communicate and be effective together as a unit. This allows for a more rounded child to be able to take these same type of life skills and use them throughout all types of scenarios in their life as they come up.

The only way to reach these types of goals is to actually be in your child's life. You can't relegate that to someone else then expect it to pop up in and out of that child's life at your convenience. I mean, that's fine when another man or woman can come in and love your child, but that child is still a part of you. No matter what you are going through personally, you have to love your child.

Also, when you don't know something, seek advice about it and if something is difficult, take a step back, don't rush into it. Give yourself a chance to think through the situation to find the best fix for the issue at hand. A lot of times when you don't follow through or you rush and don't get it right, then history will most definitely repeat itself. It may be repeated through you, or even through your child as an adult. In parenting remember that kids pick up any and everything that they hear and see. You have to do like Kool Moe Dee said, 'put a stain in your brain that will remain.' That stain would be values. Take your time to teach and love. You have to put it in for it to come out.

GROWING UP

I had a very happy childhood. I grew up with four siblings (three sisters and one brother), with me being right in the middle having two before and two after me. I grew up in the Midwest. Our entire childhood was consistent of a family-oriented lifestyle. We were all into some type of sports throughout the year. We played baseball, basketball, and football throughout the year. Even my sisters were playing sports too.

My parents were both there as we were growing up. They were married for sixty-three years until my dad passed away.

MEMORIES

My most negative experience was from culture shock. In my hometown, I was used to an all-Black neighborhood surrounded by church and church families two doors down from our house. Our neighbors would not hesitate to tell us "you know you are not supposed to be down this far" or "get back down the street." I was just really used to being around "our people". I would see White people on TV, but it wasn't in my neighborhood or where my paths went. Although I think that helped me the most was that we moved to California. It was a variety of people and that was my first exposure to different people (Mexicans, Chinese and White people). That was real eye opening for me because all that I had ever known was Black and Native American people and a few white people. I knew them just from seeing them in their cars driving around going somewhere.

My dad eventually moved us out from there to here on the east coast. When I was in elementary school in the fourth grade we moved into an all-White neighborhood. Needless to say, I hated it. The only Black people in the school were me and my three sisters. My brother was already in high school, so it didn't affect him in the same way with us. He did have to put up with some more blatant racism because he was thrust into an environment with sons and daughters of White generals and admirals in the military.

I can remember my first day of school and it being such a big impact on me. Knowing that I was the only Black boy in the along with my sisters. When I walked into the classroom, it was like I was moving in slow motion. It was as if someone had broken something and everybody turned and looked at me. As I was walking through the door I was like "wow" and thought let me get to a chair and sit down. It was an experience and it still kind of resonates with me right now. It was simply because they didn't want me there. That situation messed me up because my world was Black and at that moment it no longer was. I never had to think about any of that stuff. Just simply being a kid and it changed that day. Then as time went on, I just learned how to deal with it. As I got older and still the only Black people in the school until the sixth grade and we didn't click. I thought we would, but we didn't. Then I went to junior high which was a good experience. I also started learning that just because you are Black it doesn't mean anything. That was my world as a kid. Black was everything.

During my elementary school years, there was actually one White kid that befriended me. He invited me to his house on a number of occasions. Back then, my mom had to make sure to meet his parents and have a slight conversation with them in order to feel them out. This also ensured her that I was going to be in a "safe place" amongst a family that came from the other side. He and I actually became good friends, and this has enabled us to secure a bond that I have been able to cherish until this day. On top of that, my mom and his mom became very close through the years, and they are still friends and keep in contact as well to this day. My mom has recently received a Happy Birthday video from them.

By the time I was in junior high it was a different ball game. It became, "oh you know too many white people." I would ask my Black friends what they were talking about, and they would respond to me, "oh you're White." So, then that was a battle. So, then I had to make sure that I was showing to the Black community that I was genuine just like I had shown the White people. I could only be me. I had to learn not to worry about anyone else and that's the way things went.

I was able to meet what I didn't know at the time, would be, two of my closest friends. They used to talk all kinds of junk to me when we played ball against one another during school games. They lived in the City while I was still in the County. It was great and I loved it. Playing sports against one another and talking mess to one another was fine. They used to tease me and say, "why don't you stop playing with those White boys and come play with us." That didn't bother me because we were playing. It was good banter because we were playing sports and that's what we do when we are playing ball.

Once I got to high school. One of my friends ended up going to the same high school as I was attending. Our friendship grew from there and continues to grow to this day. That was a negative situation that did end up with a positive outcome. It taught me how to learn how to deal with people and understanding that people have their own issues, and it really doesn't have anything to do with you. That was the most positive thing that happened in my early days after our move from the Midwest to California then to what I know now to

195

be my home. It grounded me and enabled me to look at people for who they were and not just for the color of their skin. I always just figured that when you were Black that you just fit in with Black people and that was it. As a kid you didn't think about all that other stuff. You also don't realize that when you are a kid and your inability to handle anger, or your emotions will eventually place you in situations to deal with racism that prompts you to act differently than lashing out. You grow from these various incidences and then one day you look up and see that life has put you in a position to better understand and deal with people of all races.

Over time, when I was younger I found out that my behaviors that I showed when I was younger was somewhat parallel to how my dad used to act when he was younger. Yet, growing up and getting those feelings under control has allowed me to stay on the good side of freedom because at that time, had I decided to act out, I would have more than likely ended up behind bars. I had to learn to take on a different persona. I truly believe that because my dad was in our lives that helped with being able to make those changes. My dad didn't say a whole lot but when he did speak, everybody listened. My mom may be screaming and yelling at the kids and then dad would come in and just simply say, "hey!" At that point, that one word ended everything that was going on inclusive of any chaos. I thank my dad for a number of things, such as taking us to church. He used to do bible study with us when we were little kids. He helped us with all of our homework and any projects. He was right there in the midst of it all. He always told us that we have to be better than the next person. You don't have the same opportunities as they do, and you just have to do double the work. He would always say "you can't do what they do because you will end up in jail and they will be at home."

Even though my dad took us out to the West coast and then over to the East coast, he would make sure holidays or whatever, he would take us to see our relatives in the Midwest. He would do that twenty-hour drive in our station wagon to make sure that we kept not only the traditions alive but our family relationships together. My uncles played a big part in showing me good traits like working hard and ensuring you give your elders respect. My dad was such a strong family man that he would take us back in order for us to spend the summer with our relatives. This allowed us to not just keep family first but to create those strong bonds with our cousins. Back I those days we could only write letters and we as kids weren't doing any of that. The only other option we had at our disposal would be to make a phone call and it was a long-distance call then. There were no cell phones or free long-distance communication. There was no contact. We always looked for to those holidays and summer visits. We are now doing the same things now with our nieces and nephews and they in turn do the same thing as cousins. It's just good to see that happening amongst them.

I completed high school and went to college. My best friend and I used to talk about attending a well-known HBCU in the City but opted out of doing so in the long run. I am glad we made the decision not to go there. I ended up going to a private college in another state while he went to a different school in another state. It turned out for me to be a blessing to be able to move away from here at that time. It allowed me to meet different people. Which I have always said that where I grew up with the racism made it so much easier for me in the long run to be able to meet and accept new people for who they are. I worked hard and received my degree in Human Services/Sociology. I thought I was going to be a football coach but that didn't happen. When I got out of school my best friend was already on the West coast, so he

197

encouraged me to come out there and get a job and I agreed. I went out there for a little while. Was I looking for a job? Not really. However, my sister was in a nearby state, and she suggested I come there and get a place so she could move with me and finish school. I agreed to that. One of my uncles, who I looked up to, was out there and was in charge of one of the correctional schools. He helped me to secure employment, secured housing and my sister finished school. Unfortunately, after this occurred my dad ended up having quadruple bypass. I realized that I was too far away for my liking and made the decision to return back home to where my family was.

Upon returning home, I was not working in my field. I was actually working with a moving company. I not only worked for the guy that owned the company, but he would also let me and two of my closest friends use his truck to move furniture on our own off the clock. I even remember the three of us using one of his trucks and taking furniture on a road trip up North to one of my friends' sister who was there in college.

I eventually found a job with the County within the court system. I didn't think I was going to be there that long at the beginning. However, I ended up being there for almost thirty-three years. I was able to retire from there at a young age. That job was a blessing too. I didn't know what I had going into it. The pension plan and everything they offered was not something that I was familiar with. It was about ten years into time with them and people were telling me how I shouldn't leave the County. Then I started looking into it more and educating myself on that type of stuff. Of course, after some conversations and looking at what possibilities I could be set up with for my future I decided I would stay. It was such a good set up that the age I am now, I can relax and stay home and be there for my son. I am young enough to enjoy myself and not to have to worry about the lifestyle that is beneficial to my family and myself. I recommend everyone to look into whatever their employer has and take advantage of it. I had so many plans to do different things after retirement, but I retired in March of 2020. On that Friday everything was shut down. This allowed me to be able to stay home and reevaluate the list of things I originally had put together in my head. Moving my schedule around for my loved ones to include checking on my mom daily is just one of the highlights of being retired. I have always made sure we talked over the phone but now I am able to go and lay eyes on her and this means a great deal to me.

BECOMING A FATHER

I will be married for fifteen years as of October 2023. Everybody always thought that I wasn't going to get married. We started with a long-distance relationship. I say she was stalking me lol. We traveled a lot and some of my friends and I were up North during a ski trip and that is when my wife said she first saw me. However, on another occasion at an Essence Festival one of my friends stopped my not-yet wife and her girlfriends and told them, "y'all can't go pass us unless y'all hug us." At that time my, she looks at me and says, "I know you from somewhere" and of course my response was, "you don't know me, don't be playing that." So, we go back and forth debating whether we know one another or not. It wasn't until later that day we ran into them again and we ran into them again and she asks me was I from another state and did I go skiing. We realized that we had seen one another previously (because she doesn't forget faces). That's how we started our dating for the first couple of years.

Eventually I asked her to marry me, and we did so when I was forty-nine years old. Up until that point I didn't think that I was going to get married, and I definitely didn't think I was going to have any kids. I just was not going to have kids for the sake of having them with anybody. We had been trying to get pregnant, but we ran into some rough spots. We found ourselves dealing with the age factor first then there were some pregnancy-related obstacles that led to a miscarriage.

We went through those trials and tribulations and then God blessed us with our son. We were elated of course when we found out that she was pregnant. At first, finding out that I was going to finally be a father I was filled with so much joy. I was on a natural high. Going through the pregnancy the doctors informed us that there may end up being some medical concerns with the baby. Once this news came from the doctors I came crashing down. So naturally, we prayed, and we were blessed. Yes, he is a special needs kid, but I can truly say that he is the joy of my heart. He keeps me laughing and with a smile on my face. Sometimes I tell him that I would like to get up inside of his head because of some of the things that he comes up with. He is an awesome kid. I never would have thought how much awesomeness could come from one human being. It's a beautiful thing.

I think the hardest thing that I have had to deal with in raising my son has been myself being ready to jump and fight for him. I think that may be with any parent. Especially when you think your child is not being included in something. I have experienced it myself. Since my son is just a happy kid, I don't know how he takes things in. I have just noticed how people look at him as if he has some type of disease or as if he is not human. You even see it from the other kids and their behaviors toward him. Then you finally get to meet some of their parents and the light bulb goes on and I see where the kids are getting their reactions from. You can't really take it out on the kids, but you do have a feeling of wanting to yank them up right quickly. Yet you have to understand that they are learning this from some adult. It's not generally the nature of kids. Even little kids love my son and want to be with him. I go on field trips with my son, and I see his interaction with other kids. Some of them all over him and making sure that he is where he is supposed to be. That does put joy into my heart to know that these kids are looking out for him. I can constantly hear them calling him, directing him to come and do something with them. That has been a blessing in itself. It's just that in the back of your head that you wonder what's going on in your absence. I know he won't come home and say, "hey daddy this kid or adult this to me." I am always thinking about that scenario and making sure that he is okay.

My son is verbal. I can usually tell when there is something wrong or bothering him because his demeanor changes. Normally he is a smiling, laughing, very happy kid but when something happens it's almost as if it sucks his energy out of him. He can sometimes tell you when something is going on but then there are times when you have to do a lot of coaching. You just have to ask the right question and so on if something is going on. It is pretty much the same as if you were dealing with a child who would be considered on target without any challenges.

In dealing with a child with challenges my wife and I have to bounce things off one another surrounding our son's educational goals. We have to remain intentional about whatever goals that we would like to see worked on in school. It is not just about what the educators want or feel that he should be capable of doing. We as his parents find ourselves pushing, leading and just as vocal for him as they are. This year we have had to be even more present and advocate for his needs due to the changes in staffing within his classroom. When his day-to-day schedule changes and as the adults do things differently, he has a difficult time making adjustments to new routines and he shows more of what is considered negative behaviors.

My family and friends who have kids have been a great blueprint for me as a parent. I have seen how they operated and some of my friends may not have wanted or did not have any say in parenting. That part is confusing to me because I can't imagine how a dad can easily accept that mindset of not being involved. I just can't wrap my head around that because that wasn't in the realm of my family. My dad and all of my uncles were all involved in raising their children. I watched everybody and I took what I needed from each person that I watched. I didn't have anyone that I could talk to or have mentor me in the aspect of raising a child with special needs. After thinking about it in the early years, I realized that I just needed to be his dad. That's what he needed was for me to be his dad.

GENERATIONAL TRAITS

I think that I have carried the disciplinarian trait from my dad into my parenting. With him, it was A, B & C. There was no D, E & F with him. I know that I bring that same mindset in with my son. I think that my wife and other members of my family are starting to understand that he is just a regular kid, and you can't let him just get away with anything that he wants to. People think that I am hard anyway. Especially with my past employment where I worked with kids. I was a matter-of-fact guy with them, and I am kind of the same way with my son. My dad didn't say much but you knew where he stood on a lot of things. You knew what you could get away with and what you couldn't get away with. That's how I am with my son. I may have to say a lot more than my dad did. My dad could just raise his head a certain way and you knew that you were about to get it or knew that you were about to put it in reverse.

I have noticed that my son looks at me to see if I am mad, happy, or whatever before he does something. If he knows that I'm smiling and laughing then he knows he can get away with just about anything. He knows that and I realize that he knows that. My wife tells me that I'm just a sucker for him and he has me on a string. That's not it, because he listens to me when I say something or give him directions. He may be sulky, but he follows through with what I am telling. I think I bring that from my childhood. When I was growing up mom would be yelling and screaming and we all would be ducking and dodging yet when dad comes home, everything comes to a complete stop. Don't get me wrong because my mom was a disciplinarian too. She got us but she was more verbal. As kids we knew that she was more into talking and that we could get away with whatever antics we had going on and how far we could push things. Sometimes she would go on and on and want us to hear whatever it was that she needed to say to make sure that we understood. She was the opposite of my dad.

So needless to say, I didn't pick up the trait from my mom. I received my dad's state of mind of not having or wanting to say a whole lot about the situation. In order to get your point across people have to know where you stand and not wishy washy. That is what I bring to my parenting with my son. He knows where I stand and how far he can truly push things. I learned that from my dad. Even when I was working with the juvenile population at my job, some of the older guys used to always complement me and tell me that I was going to be a great parent when the time came. I used to tell them that I wasn't sure if I was going to have kids because if I didn't find the right woman it was going to happen. I do believe thought, with me just watching what my dad did with us as we were growing up, parenting just seemed natural to me. Also, because you know your child is watching you and seeing the good, bad, positive, and negative in everything that you are doing. They are taking it all in.

I really don't remember anything that I saw or picked up from my dad that may have been negative. If I had to say anything, I can say that at one time he did smoke some big cigars and a pipe because his dad did. As little kids, we used to tell him that he didn't need to be smoking and he stopped. There was not any types of behaviors from drinking or cussing that I witnessed that I could have actually taken on and made a part of my life as not just as an adult but as a parent.

WORDS OF WISDOM

Enjoy it. Embrace it. Enjoy every little thing about parenting. Even the little milestones. Don't worry about making a mistake because you will. Just focus on being positive with everything you do with your child. Whatever that may be. Take everything as a blessing. You are responsible for a life. So be a good and positive example for your child. You have the opportunity to mold someone and start them on a good life journey.

I grew up in the house with both of my parents present. They were married forty-four years, until my mom passed away about two years ago. There were three children born from their union, two sons and a daughter. I was a middle child. I would say that I had a happy childhood.

My siblings and I got along well. I am three years older than my younger sister and had a little more friction with her. She used to run away often. My brother, however, is like five and a half years older than me. By the time I started paying attention, he was always doing something and barely in the house. He would sleep in the house but by the time I got older he was away at school, and I was in middle school. So as an older brother to me, I don't really remember him as a child. With the age difference he had his own friends and activities he was into and that kept him outside of the house a lot of times.

Growing up I did not have any type of discipline in my life. I never received any type of whooping. I was pretty quiet though. I kept to myself a lot and enjoyed doing puzzles. There was never a situation when it was "my fault." As a child I was babied, but I was still a mature child. The first time I left home, I was around fifteen years old.

I graduated high school at the age of seventeen. I never attended one of the neighborhood schools like my siblings. My parents did not allow me to do so because of the early negative influences I picked up on outside of the house. This made me more aware of my surroundings and the individuals around me from my mother's side of the family, which in turn led me to be more street savvy. There was a bout with trouble that I found myself in while I was in the ninth grade. It really wasn't my fault, but I ended up going to a private school. During the time that I attended private school, I found that my studies were much farther along than when I was in the public school system. Upon my return to public schools, it was backwards. I had already taken the courses for the 11th and 12 grades. I found out that assignments and the curriculum that was being given to me I had already taken during the time I was in the private school. I was enrolled in more college courses at that time.

When I returned to public school it was very different because I was around people who were not like me. It was a problem or rather an adjustment. I felt very much like an outsider. I felt welcomed but at the same time I felt like I was pointed out. Like if I made a mistake, you knew I made that mistake. It was like I was singled out very easily.

I completed high school, graduated, and then went into the military. I enlisted into the Navy and completed a four-year tour. My first duty I was stationed up North and that was the best time I had in my life. We traveled and had fun. We were just assigned to do a job and then do whatever it was we wanted to after that. Eventually the base was closed, and I was transferred. I found it to be more political there. It was a big difference between the two bases. Up North, we really didn't have to salute on our base. We knew who the officers were, and they knew who we were. It was just that type of relationship. However, when we got to the more Southern base, the political aspect was more prominent as in 'you know who I am, and you are supposed to salute me.' It was a big drastic change and it made me not like it any longer.

When I first enlisted, I did seven months away from the United States and I had never been away. I had never been out of town before then. That was uncomfortable to me. I came back and I was here for about a month only to leave again for about six months. Then I just happened to be back home when 9-11 occurred. After that, the next two years I was away on the water. I did three Mediterranean (Med) cruises and on my first ship we hit a lot of different ports. After that everything was on high alert, and we were not able to have the freedom to do whatever we wanted to. We were very limited and in turn that took the fun and excitement out of it all for me. It was at that time, after dealing with politics, along with my young age, I decided to come home and not re-enlist. I can say that I have no regrets about not re-enlisting, and I am comfortable with the decision that I made.

The occupation that I am doing now stems from planning on doing it and just falling into it. The choice does come from the strained relationship that I have from my mother's side of the family. They have always had these types of companies within this field and while I was young, I used to want to work with them. One of them would allow me to work with them, but the others that were doing very well with their business would always look past me and hire outside of our circle. Being a handyman when I was younger was something that I wanted to always do but did not have access to anyone who would teach me the ropes. As the years went by, I just started teaching myself. Now I have a wide range of skills ranging from carpentry to home remodeling and more where I am self-employed.

BECOMING A FATHER

While I was in the military and about the age of twenty-one years, I found out I was going to be a father. I was having an on/off relationship with a young lady whenever I returned from the ship to home. I was at sea more time than I was on land so it always a brief encounter. It was not a serious relationship, but we had known one another for several years

209

platonically. Initially, I was shocked when I was told that she was expecting. The shock was due to the mere fact that the pregnancy came about quickly. When I say fast, I mean, I did a Med cruise, came home one weekend, left and then three months later I got a call.

The night she was having the baby, I was up North when she called me while I was out. I made my way by catching a bus to the hospital down South. It was at that time I said to myself, "oh this is real, she's having her." While she was having her, I found another level of shock because I had never experienced anything like that. So, when I got my opportunity and the doctor told me to get some ice, it took me a long time to come back.

I never married the mother of my first daughter. We were not together in a relationship by the time our daughter was born. However, her mother and I were very good friends initially and we always said that she and I should never have gotten into a relationship at all.

At first the co-parenting was a little rough. We were both young and didn't get along at first. She went away to school, and I was in the military and when I came home when the baby was two. It was hard to figure out, I just know that our relationship was a strain. To make matters a bit more complex, once I came home, she was having another baby. It was ironic at that point, the two of us found our ability to communicate better with one another. I showed up, held her baby and from that point on we were able to talk. That's how we became friends again. Everything just moved forward and we're friends to this day. We may not agree on a lot of issues, but we are able to talk about it without arguing.

I have four other children who have the same mother. Before we had any children we worked together in the military.

Legally, we were not supposed to have any type of relationship with one another at all. We were cool though. We had the same group of friends. I wouldn't consider it a relationship; it was more of a friendship. What I will say is I like women and I had a lot of female friends, and she was one of them. I was not looking to settle down. I got out of the military in 2003 and the next time I spoke to her was in 2005, when she was stationed at a base closer to home. That's how we reconnected when she called because I never changed my number. I was back home, comfortable and feeling good about where I was with myself. I ignored her for a few months until one night I decided to meet up with her. I slept with her once in 2006 and it was almost the same storyline as my previous situation. I got a call and she said she was pregnant.

The tricky part comes with me finding out that she was pregnant because I was already in what I felt was a committed relationship. I had to break this news. I had to admit that I made a mistake, and this is the result of it. This, of course, was not received well and ended the relationship. I did not immediately go into a relationship with the expecting mother of my child. It was after the baby was born that I decided to do so. I was in my mid-twenties, so it was around the time that I was starting to slow down and calming down some of my other activities. In 2007, about six months or so after this we married one another. I didn't feel obligated to marry her and I had known her for about eight years. So, it wasn't as if she someone I just met, we knew one another to a certain extent. I never gave it a lot of thought. I would suppose it was just the timing of everything. I didn't marry her because I was concerned about the court system or having to pay any type of child support to her. I believe it was more of me being at my "growing up" moment. Four years later we had another child together and three years later we had a set of twins.

Most of the disciplinary responsibilities fell on my wife. Our household was a little different. Even though she was supposedly 'in charge' of the kids, a lot of times I would have to get on her and she would have to get on the kids. It would trickle down. To say whether it was by force or choice, she had a choice or an option, but I would kind of have to force her to take care of the house. This was during the time when we had the first two. On most occasions, I will say this, when I was at work; I was at work and when I was home, I was at work. I always had to stay on top of something and I still do to this day because nothing will get done if I don't say anything.

Our communication would flow easily if I were at home. I would say something to her to get something done and then I would know it would be done. However, if I was away from home, communication wasn't easy at all. For example, I would ask, "did you cook dinner already and will they be in the bed by 9:00?" She would then answer with "yes I cooked them dinner and they will be eating at 6:00." I would be like, "okay cool." Yet, when I get home about 9:00, they are about to eat. Of course, I would ask, "what happened this time?" Then it just goes from there. It wasn't true, it's just if he isn't here, I can say anything and that's the way it went. I would have to do whatever needed to be or hadn't been done to get things organized to go to sleep myself. Nothing was done by her.

I know for a fact the lack of organization and follow-through has affected the kids. Even to this day, I will have to get on them for the basic things or stuff that they should know by now. Things from brushing their teeth daily, picking up trash around the house, I have to stay on them and watch them when they are around me. We are currently legally separated, and the divorce papers have been filed, received, and should be finalized soon. The children are at their happiest now, especially when they are spending time with me. They love spending time with me. They love us both. I don't say anything about her to them concerning our issues. I just make sure that they have a good time. The problem still is with our level of communication. Sometimes I will get mad, and I have to calm myself down, but she will use any excuse to hang up the phone on me or anything if I am saying something about what I see is wrong. I know it's confusing to the kids because they think about how they can do certain things over here but can't do it over there. Like one parent will make me clean up while the other one won't make me do anything.

While they are under my care, they receive structure and guidance and have a chance to be happy. Yet, when they are at home, they get just the opposite. Although I can see them about every weekend. Their mother is not driving at the time so it's a lot on me to go to work, then pick them up, drop them off, and do all the other things with them. This is also inclusive of all the calls I receive during the week. I will say that it is another job. I do everything for them for their household financially. I am pretty much in the dark about the responsibilities or lack thereof surrounding what she does for them. I still try to communicate with her, but it is not a back-and-forth conversation. It's one way with her just responding with a simple okay. I can truly say that there is no teamwork or co-parenting.

Concerning why there is no feedback from her when I try and reach out, I think she may be a little upset. There is a lot that we don't agree on. The way I see it, she looks forward to doing something that she knows that I won't like. I think it's just that she is against me. I feel as if she really shouldn't be if she cared about our kids.

I am not sure if she is salty because we are not still together. It's confusing to me. We have been separated for a while now, so I don't know why she acts this way toward me. This isn't new nor did it just happen, it's been this way. After not being able to communicate along with the lies for so long, I just got tired of it all. With the various situations that we found ourselves going through, it just became so easy for her to lie to me about anything. I can ask if a bill had been paid and she would tell me it had been only to find out three months later the lights would be off. At that point I would ask her about the bill being paid again and she would give me the runaround and back pedal about why it had not been done. It was just too easy for her to lie to me about things that would have a big effect on everyone. I finally had to decide that enough was enough and allow myself to take measures into my own hands to protect my sanity, growth, and my peace.

I do have a stepdaughter, a bonus daughter. My wife had a daughter prior to our union. My wife and her mother were always a little funny from the beginning regarding my relationship with my stepdaughter. She does call me daddy and is respectful. She is a nineteen-year-old teenager now and has always wanted to find her biological father. However, her mother has never been able to give her any information on that regarding who her father is. It has always been a tug-of-war with them and her.

I got a phone call from them (my wife's family) once requesting that I not say anything to my stepdaughter concerning discipline. My response of course, was "not in my house!" My stepdaughter will call when she needs something, or she will try and figure it out on her own. That is one of the bad traits she has from watching her mom. I want her to understand that I am not here to hurt you, but I am here to help you as much as I can. She has grown up being in the middle of my wife and I issues. She does tend to take her mother's side on things. I had a nice talk with her not too long ago. She was supposed to be going to school (college), yet her mother dropped the ball again. I didn't know about it until it was late, and I explained I won't know anything unless you communicate with me about it. I would love to see her go to school. However, she has some characteristics and learned behaviors that at this time are keeping her from finding her path and wanting to broaden her horizons to get away and learn something new.

I can say that I learned several things from my parents as I was growing up. One of the biggest things I carry with me is being a provider. My father took me to a lot of places with him but at the same time I was always with my mother. I am that way with my own children too. Wherever they want to go, I do whatever it takes to make it happen. I may not be the one to take them to the park or wherever, but I will provide the finances that it takes to make sure they can go. I tend not to go, but I will take them and drop them off. Just take them to the park and I will go to work. It's been like this for years.

You just figure everything is okay until you get home and realize the kids haven't been able to do the things that they were supposed to because of the lack of parental supervision. So, when I get home and find this out, I end up being the one saying okay let's hurry up and go to the mall or something. This will pacify the situation in my eyes since I have been gone and working all day. That's just how I would make up for it because at that point they would be happy. However, in the grand scheme of things that's not how I always wanted them to be. I really wanted them enrolled in activities, especially since their mom has the time to do make sure they do it. She is available timewise but not available to them.

215

If I had an opportunity to have a do-over as far as being a parent, it would have to be when I was much younger. I would have saved a lot more money. I would have thought more about the future instead of just living in the moment. That would put me in a position to be better prepared for situations like I'm going through now. I would be able to be more flexible between my home life and work. I also would have paid more attention to the individual(s) I chose to have kids with. I would pay more attention and listen more instead of having that 'know-it-all' mentality. Especially since I grew up fast when I was young.

TODAY IN SOCIETY

As far as society playing a big part in children growing up, my kids are big fans of games. I feel as if they do it a little bit too much. I may send them outside and they will be out for five minutes and shoot the basketball with them and then the complaints start. They say, "it's too hot" and other things. It does aggravate me because I grew up outside. They are the opposite of that. However, my youngest daughter is cool with having a social life. She has her friends and is always getting invited to parties or having sleepovers or something. Now that's something that I didn't do when I was growing up, but I am comfortable with the area that she is in and the people around that she is associated with. So, she is good, and she is her own independent mama. Sometimes I do notice that she is the mama of the bunch. She tries to make it make sense to her brothers. I may take them to a jump place on Saturday and then they may give me a suggestion for something else. I then explain well we can't do both at the same time. Being the voice of reason, it's then that my daughter will chime in and suggest since we had a good time yesterday, let's have a good time and eat. She is always watching them too and I try to give her a little space when she is with me. She is the one with her own room and privacy, so I believe I am doing the right thing.

Now her older sister, by my first daughter's mother, is about to be twenty-one. So, every opportunity when she is not working, she is always willing to give suggestions and ideas for us to do together. She gets me going and motivated to go out with them as well. She is very helpful to me with that, and she also enjoys it herself.

My mother was a big support to me before she passed about two years ago. She was my entire support system. After that, no one else has been involved to the point I would say they are my support. In short, my children were visiting somewhere, and I was called and told that the adult could tell they had not been getting a bath. As a dad, of course, I immediately leave work and drive to where they are at the time to give them a bath. Yet, if my mother were still alive, I would not had even known this to be true at all because she would have taken care of bathing them, had them Vaseline up and sleep. That's the big difference.

MEMORIES

Some of my fondest memories of growing up were with my mom. I did everything with her. I would go to the mall with her, pick out her clothes and she would wear the outfits and look very nice in them. I was always with her at the hairdresser, going places and I'm just having fun. The one difference I realize now that I notice that she is gone was that she is family oriented. She didn't have too many people in her house. She would help you out if you needed it, but when it came down to her immediate family, which was who she focused on. My mother was the strong one in our household.

My dad is confusing to me at times. He has moved on with his life with a new girlfriend since my mom's passing. He does things that disturb me. For example, we have had a family home for thirty years in the area still to this day. We have always had an extended family and sometimes he will give some of these individuals permission to utilize the family home for their own personal use, knowing that his grandchildren, my children are slated to come. For him to allow others to come and stay at our home for months at a time knowing that it is used by your immediate family on a regular basis confuses the heck out of me. This is the big difference between my parents. My mom would make sure she kept with the program and that her immediate priority was taken care of first.

WORDS OF WISDOM

Always keep in mind that it is going to be some hard work and you are not going to agree on everything. You are going to have to put the work in and be understanding. If you have an issue, you must learn how to communicate about it and getting on the same page. If you have wants and needs express them, but also listen to your other half. That's what is really important; to be on the same page. Make your goals and follow them through. It's kind of hard to talk to the youth these days because they know everything and are very opinionated. You must still talk with them, and you don't want to upset them, but you must at some times and in certain situations. You must always respect a female even if you do not see eye to eye. You will know if you have a good woman when you have one. It's about respect and sometimes you must change your ways. Some people do it sooner than others. You will at some point have to make some sacrifices and compromises.

"SIMPSON"

GROWING UP

As a child growing up, it was mainly my mother and my older sister. My mother ran a great household and set boundaries early on for both my sister and me. She ensured that we were happy, healthy, and well-mannered children.

We didn't move around that much. As a single parent, my mom made sure that we were exposed to everything possible. My sister and I got along really good, and we were always looking out for one another. Our differences came in as normal siblings, where I was into sports, and she was into books. She did, however, play volleyball for a while and the flute. As for myself, I played the saxophone but as I stated, I was mainly into sports.

Initially, my dad was around. My parents were married for about nineteen years. Unfortunately, he found himself in some trouble, went away for a while and at some point, he and my mom divorced. After that, once he returned to the area, he was more so in and out of our lives. We would see him for a while and then we wouldn't see him. I can say that when he was around, he was a good dad. He made sure that he provided for us and that we had what we needed when he was in the picture. He made sure that he tried to remain a good role model for me. I can't speak for my sister but, for me, he made every attempt to be there for me. He always instilled in me to be strong and not to take no mess from nobody. One of the biggest things he used to tell me was, "you gotta go get what you want" and "if you want it, then you gotta work for it."

Sometime after my parents divorced, my dad remarried, and they had two children who are about twenty years or so younger than I am. I have a sister and a brother in addition to my sister from my mom. The four of us get along very well with one another. We are in contact with each other regularly. When we were younger, my mom always ensured and encouraged my oldest sister and I to reach out to our two younger siblings to make sure that they were okay. This direction from my mom has helped all of us to secure a very tight relationship amongst the four of us.

<u>*MEMORIES*</u>

In growing up, I used to see my parents not getting along. Everybody has seen their parents in disagreements, arguing or fighting. Our household was no different. I saw mine do it and it stayed with me and made a big impact on me, and it stuck with me for a long time. I vowed to myself to not want certain things in my relationships when I got older.

Remembering the positive things that happened in my life, there are a number of things that stick out to me. One of the things I loved a lot was how my mom took us traveling. We went on vacations to places that we may not have normally gone to. She wanted to expose us to as much as she possibly could and put forth the effort needed to make things happen. As a child there was always a summer vacation planned well in advance of us finishing the school year. We also went on many trips together. One of my favorite trips was to the NFL Hall of Fame (because we were a sports-oriented family). That's a trip that has always stayed in my mind.

As I was growing up my mom showed me what it meant to have strong work ethics. She worked countless hours without complaining. She was employed at a well-known, privately owned food supply chain of stores, where she climbed the chain of command from District Manager to Regional Manager to Director of Processing and Director of

Administration over a good number of stores and employees. I can proudly say that not only did she instill those same ethics into us, but my sister and I hold on to it to this day. She made sure to lay down a blueprint of having to work for anything I want or need and not waiting for someone to give it to me. By ensuring that strong core values were poured into my sister and I, the both of us have done relatively well in our careers. My oldest sister of course graduated from a university that is consistently placed in the top 20 colleges. She worked extremely hard as well to obtain her M.D. and has been a pediatrician for the last thirty-five years. That simple yet powerful concept has taken us far in my life.

Going back to how my mom always made sure that we were as well rounded as possible. She made sure that school and chores were things that were first before any other activities. I am thankful for those things too (even though no kid likes it when we are being told to do it). With her loving heart, and pointing us toward our siblings, she helped the four of us to create bonds that we more than likely would never have since we didn't grow up in the same household. Albeit one would think we did. Especially my sisters. I say this because we would have never thought that our dad's daughters would both end up being doctors. My youngest sister is the CEO of her own mental health counseling group.

Growing up I was faced with moments when I was sad because my dad was not around. During his absences, I was faced with a void of a father-son relationship. Not having my dad in my life on a consistent basis truly affected me in the sense of not having a man I could go and talk to about my problems that I faced surrounding male issues. Fortunately, I was able to talk to my mom about certain things. She didn't always get what I was saying but she most definitely gave me the best advice that she could from her (a woman/mother's) viewpoint. With as much that she could offer to me as a parent, I did still from time to time miss that part of having that father or father-figure in my life to help me through some situations that I had in my life. When you don't have a father in your life as a young boy or man growing up, you tend to miss out on some good life lessons. The kind of lessons that teaches a young boy or an adolescent the how-to's of life.

My mom never remarried. She had male friends that were nice, but, as a young man, I just never connected enough with them in that manner. I have one uncle who is my mom's younger brother. He tried to fill the void sometimes when he was not away in school or even busy with his own family matters. As far as me having anyone else that would or even could step up to the plate, that's a negative. I played sports during my school years and with that comes male figures that happened to be my coaches. I did learn a few things from them in respect to being a young man. Those coaches that spent countless hours with me during both football and basketball were hands-on with me during and after practices and sporting events.

I went to school in the city I was born in from elementary through high school. Growing up I started playing football and basketball when I was in elementary school. In addition to playing for the school teams, I started playing at the area recreation centers. By the time I was in Jr. High school, I found my best skills stood out as a quarterback. It was there the undefeated (10-0) team I was playing with won the championship in 1978. That team was the last junior varsity team to win a championship before the school zones changed. As a high school player, I continued to play both sports. However, the basketball team I played on was undefeated and we made it to the State semi-finals where we lost in the first round in 1979-80.

I graduated from high school in 1981. Afterward, I attended a four-year college and graduated with a degree in Sociology and a minor in Business. Along with attending college, I was fortunate to join a fraternity that has afforded me lifelong friendships. This brotherhood is like no other and our bonds have extended up to this very day. I needed that experience of going away to college in my life to grow up. I wasn't around my mom or anyone else that was close to me. It made me learn to become independent and take some initiative on things.

While I was away in school, I of course had my mom and my aunts that supported me. Each of them would always send me money whenever I needed it. Every now and then I would look up and there would be something in the mailbox. It would be twenty-five or fifty dollars that I had not asked for. They just knew that I needed it for something I may need in school to try and help me out. I also had my oldest sister that supported me every now and then, but she was in school herself. We were right behind one another with only one year separating the two of us. She would always encourage me to keep going and not to give up. So, I definitely had a good support system behind me. I definitely appreciated it and will never forget the sacrifices they made for me to be able to accomplish my goals.

I am currently a Shift Supervisor with a large food company. This job was not my goal or ideal position at the onset of my employment. In my high school years, I just knew that I was going to be a master printer but that did not work out. So, fortunately with my background with my college degree, I am able to bring to the company a unique perspective in dealing with employees. Within this position, I am able to use my sociology degree because it deals with human behavior. My education also affords me the ease of

225

supervising a large number of ethnic backgrounds, which in itself has been proven to be a challenging feat for others.

The career that I have now was not actually a backup plan. I actually stumbled into it. One day years ago, a friend of mine came to me and told me that the company he was working at had an opening and made the suggestion that I apply for it. I did just that and started working there shortly thereafter. After about two or three years I was promoted to an Area Lead position. I worked in that position for several more years and then was promoted to my current position of Shift Supervisor. In this position I do everything that entails ensuring my staff follows all the company regulations, USDA regulations, training, evaluation, conflict resolution (to say the least) and more. Again, with my work ethics I walked into the position and learned everything that I possibly could, maintained an average of zero days taken off for years and I have been employed with this company for about sixteen or seventeen years.

BECOMING A FATHER

I was about twenty-two years old when I first found out that I was going to be a father. I had been messing around with this girl for about a year and she got pregnant. Initially, I was scared and didn't know if I could do a good job. Taking the time to look back on my childhood and my father and didn't want to do the same thing to my kid. So, I made the effort to make sure that I was in her life. I was more nervous than anything because I didn't know what to do. I decided to marry my child's mother, because I just could not see myself (or my child) having to go through the court system dealing with anything pertaining to child support or visitation, etc. We ended up during our marriage with a total of three daughters.

All three of my children are adults now. One of my daughters is currently in school working on her doctorate degree. The other two are working and financially on their own and supporting themselves. None of them have any children, therefore I do not have any biological grandchildren. They have grown up to have their own values and work hard. I believe they have taken that from me which stems from me being in their lives consistently while growing up. I always vowed that no matter what happened in my life, my marriage or anything surrounding those things, that I would be there for them and see them graduate and branch out on their own. I have accomplished that goal as well.

The marriage between their mother and I ended in divorce. She and I do not have any type of relationship much less any level of communication with one another. It was years prior to our divorce that she and I had any type of relationship. As with most things, long term once ended, it can be difficult to start over. What has enabled me to keep my head up and move forward is the fact that I kept my promise to my children and myself in making sure I was there for them to the best of my ability.

My support system while my children were growing up consisted of several people. My mom was always there if I or any of them needed something. She and my ex did not get along. My dad was there when he was able to. My ex-wife's father was deceased, but her mother was very supportive of our relationship. There was of course her older sisters that would help out from time to time. I definitely had a support system from both sides of our family.

I have since remarried to someone who I knew from my youth, and we somewhat dated when we were younger. However, the relationship never had an opportunity to reach its' potential before we went our separate ways. Thankfully as we all get older life can give you the chance to get things right and to experience the genuine love that each of us deserves. I now have two bonus adult daughters and four bonus grandchildren. I would like to think that I have been influential in their lives as well. What has made this transition into my second marriage coupled with added family members is that my bonus children and their children have shown me nothing but love from day one. They are very well mannered and have never come at me with any type of disrespect. Our ability to communicate with one another is great. They are always open to anything that I feel needs to be addressed, just as I am when they have the need to talk with me about something. I have not run into any type of challenges with them. I have always told them, just as I let my biological children know, if you need me, I'm there or if you need something, let me know.

GENERATIONAL TRAITS

I can't say enough about this trait that I have copied and carried from watching my mom because it is one of the most important ones that I have ever learned. Watching her be diligent in her work ethics and how she treated others is what I copied and made a part of who I am. In thinking about how she showed me, I was able to show the same things to my daughters. If you want something, you have to go out here and earn it for yourself. It's rough out here in this world and things cost, so without a job if you mismanage your money then you won't have anything. My mom was a strong believer in this theory, and I have made it a foundation in my life as well.

My dad used to always tell me that my word was worth more than anything that you have. He made sure to instill in me that whatever I say, if I didn't do anything else, keep my word. If I promised my children something make sure to follow through. If I said, I was going to be there, then show up. Anything concerning my character in itself would be the best impression that I could leave. If my actions don't line up with my words then my character will have a stain on it. So, I have always tried to remain as true to my word as possible and that is something that I have too passed on to my daughters.

TODAY IN SOCIETY

Society now is really different from when I was growing up. Everything is about the value of money and costs a lot more. Social media is out of control, and I stay away from it all together. It's a big difference all around. You have to make sure that you understand that you are dealing with a child and break things down to make sure they understand it. There were a lot of things that I tried to tell my daughters about when they were growing up and they didn't understand. However, now they have come to me and said 'oh Dad, I understand what you mean now; I didn't understand what you were trying to say to me or to get me to do when I was a teen. I understand it now though.' I have told them "yes you may have felt as if I was being hard on you at that time, but I was trying to groom you for later in life because things are forever changing, and you never know what to expect." I wanted to make sure that you at least had some idea of how to handle any situation that you may be faced with when it comes to you.

REGRETS OR DO-OVER

Early on, I got involved with drugs for a while. Even though this occurred and not to minimize my wrongdoings, I was still working each and every day and doing my best to provide not just for my substances but the household as well. I got sidetracked and it hurt all involved. My oldest daughter was the only one that it affected. Let me rephrase that and say that she was the only one that was old enough to somewhat understand what was going on. Whether it had been through my behaviors or lack thereof or the conversations and arguments that resonated through the house between her mother and me. That timeframe is the one aspect that I would change or would do differently than I had done. It was not pleasant at all. It took a while, but I got out of it before my next set of daughters were old enough to understand what was going on. That is the one thing that I would go back to and change in my life.

I feel as if I did the best that I could throughout the time that my children were growing up. From the beginning until they each graduated either high school or college, I was there. Did I do everything right? I sure did not. Would I go back and change some things? Yes, I would. I would like to think overall that me being there had a positive impact on them and their lives.

RED FLAGS/FEARS

The fears I had stemmed around having and raising three daughters and worrying that they would wind up coming home pregnant. By the grace of God, neither one of them did. That was a blessing for me as a father. That in itself was my only fear that plagued me while they were growing up. I think every parent has that worry at one point or another of having to raise their child along with a grandchild.

CHALLENGES

My biggest challenge was how I looked in front of my kids. Did I do everything right for my kids? Am I a good dad? I didn't want them to be disappointed in me for not being a good dad. Like I said, I did get involved with drugs, but I pushed hard and made sure that I was there for them. I found myself facing some difficult decisions regarding my health versus my substance abuse and I prayed to God and asked for help and guidance from Him and promised that if He pulled me through that I would walk away from my activities that kept me away from being who He wanted me to be. Once I pulled myself out of the situation that I was in, I put forth the effort to make sure that I would never put myself or my daughters in that type of situation ever again.

WORDS OF WISDOM

My main piece of advice is to keep your eyes on your goals. Don't get sidetracked with society because it can affect the whole outcome of your life. If you previously had a goal for your life before you became a parent, even if it takes longer to do it, still continue to put forth the effort. It's hard to be a parent, but it is even harder to be the person that you are as a parent with regrets. Goals can be amended so that you can not only be a good parent, but you can work on being your best you.

Don't be afraid to make some mistakes. It is inevitable for that to happen. None of us are perfect or without flaws. However, once you make a mistake, make sure you learn from it. For if you do not, then you will find yourself repeating that same mistake until you learn the lesson and pass the test. Whatever you do that trips you up, take that experience with you, keep it in your mind, remember how you felt or what it did to you and learn from it. Don't ever forget to try and teach your children to be the best they can be. Make sure they are respectful of themselves and others.

With all of the nonsense and temptations out in the world, remember your past, use it as a stepping stool and be the best person that you can be. Sometimes you have to make decisions that are not popular with everyone else but if it's true to you and is positive follow your gut. Use your common sense and remember that what you put out in the world is nine times out of ten what you will get back. Most importantly, if you are unsure of what you are doing, never, ever hesitate to reach out to another man who has shown himself worthy of providing you with direction.

There are just a few things that I would like to say to any man, young or old who is currently or even has not yet become a father. In life you will be faced with a multitude of situations and each one will be different or need a different approach to handle and conquer.

The most important thing that you can bring to the table of your fatherhood is to have lots of patience. Without it, each problem will appear to be overwhelming to you. When you decide to be a parent, patience should be your best friend. The challenges of each child will warrant different levels of patience. Make sure that you allow yourself to grow in patience as required.

Another aspect of being a good father is to be a good listener. We as adults have already lived and processed a number of things by the time we become fathers. Most times, we know exactly what a child should or should not do. However, as we are never too old to learn, we are never too old to listen to what it is that our children have to say. As long as you are teaching him/her to be respectful in explaining what they are trying to get across, then your listening skills may end up hearing something that will be more beneficial in getting your point across. You are not always right and listening to them may help the situation be ironed out much easier.

In order to build a good solid foundation for your family a father must be willing to show them love. Not just in a material aspect but by actions. Showing your family love means showing up for them whenever you can. Even if you don't want to, are tired, or busy, you must make the time for them. Supporting your child does not always mean buying them whatever they want. Spending money is not a good way to buy their affection because it does tend to send mixed signals. Make sure that you are clear on your desires of the outcome that you are seeking.

Lastly, there are no earthly perfect fathers. We all learn to deal with situations as they come. Take your time when it allows in handling anything difficult. As the child's personality comes into play as they start to figure out who they are in this world, adjust your approaches as needed. This will allow for a more well-rounded person under your supervision and guidance.

A NOTE TO MY BROTHERS

To each of you gentlemen that has entrusted me to share your story, I thank you for your transparency. I pray that even though your names remain anonymous, that you can hold your head up, release any anxieties you may have or even be able to come to terms with issues you currently have or will face in the future. I am most certain, that some young man coming behind you will read these **Letters From My Brothers** and see your story and realize that there is already some living insight regarding this parenting journey from a male's perspective. Just as our ancestors did so that we didn't have to; now you have done, so those behind you do not have to.

In opening your heart and peeling back the layers to address some of your challenges, each of you have pushed through one of your first rules that you were taught as a young boy. That is for you to suck it up and hold back your tears because boys don't cry. It was drilled in you that you were not to have any type of emotional outbursts that would deem you less than a man. By sharing your experiences, my prayer for you is that of healing, forgiveness of others and yourself as well as continued and unfettered growth.

Blessings,
Tranita A. Randolph Stephens